THE TRIALS AND TRAVELS OF WILLEM LEYEL

Asta Bredsdorff

The Trials and Travels of Willem Leyel

An Account of the Danish East India Company in Tranquebar,

1639-48

Museum Tusculanum Press
University of Copenhagen
2009

Asta Bredsdorff: *The Trials and Travels of Willem Leyel: An Account of the Danish East India Company in Tranqubar, 1639-48*

© Museum Tusculanum Press and the author, 2009
Language revision by Roda Morrison
Originally published in Danish as *Willem Leyels liv og farefulde rejse til Indien* (Museum Tusculanum Press, 1999)
Set and printed by Narayana Press, www.narayanapress.dk
ISBN 978 87 635 3023 1

Cover illustration: Ove Gjedde's fortress Dansborg in Tranquebar. Courtesy of Skokloster, Sweden

This book is published with financial support from
Konsul George Jorck og hustru Emma Jorck's Fond
VELUX FONDEN

Museum Tusculanum Press
126 Njalsgade
DK-2300 Copenhagen S
www.mtp.dk

CONTENTS

FOREWORD

It is some time since I came across the unique material to be found in Willem Leyel's and Claus Rytter's papers in The Danish State Archives in Copenhagen, Denmark. Here you can get a first-hand impression of the old Danish East India Company's activities in the first half of the seventeenth century – a piece of Danish history that suddenly comes to life when you can handle the letters and reports of the main characters and thus gain some insight into the enormous difficulties that confronted them during the long voyages to the East and the huge efforts necessary to carry on trade in foreign countries with insufficient capital and a chronic lack of men to replace the many who died or deserted. But perhaps the worst privation for the little colony at Tranquebar in southern India at this time was the lack of contact with home – the first ship from Denmark after Leyel's own arrival in 1642 did not turn up until 1669. In the intervening years the men left to direct the enterprise must often have asked themselves whether there was any point in carrying on.

In spite of the huge difficulties they faced they nevertheless elected to keep things going by whatever means came to hand – and these were not always for the squeamish. They had many problems: clashes with the local rulers, competition from other European nations, drunkenness and unruliness among the garrison, the shipwreck of several of the almost irreplaceable ships, doubts as to the best trading stations, famine resulting in a dearth of the cotton goods that formed the main staple of trade with the East Indies, from where one had to buy the spices demanded by the European nations. It is hardly to be wondered at that men could not cope under these conditions; but the will to hang on conquered, and thanks to Willem Leyel and the new leaders who came after him, the fortress of Dansborg survived on Danish hands until the arrival of a new ship twenty-seven years later.

Ove Gjedde's fortress Dansborg in Tranquebar. The painting was possibly commissioned by Leyel or Crappé as propaganda for the Company. It has been surmised that the nearest of the four ships in the road might be the *Christianshavn*. (Photo: Jens Mohr. The painting can be seen at Skokloster, Sweden.)

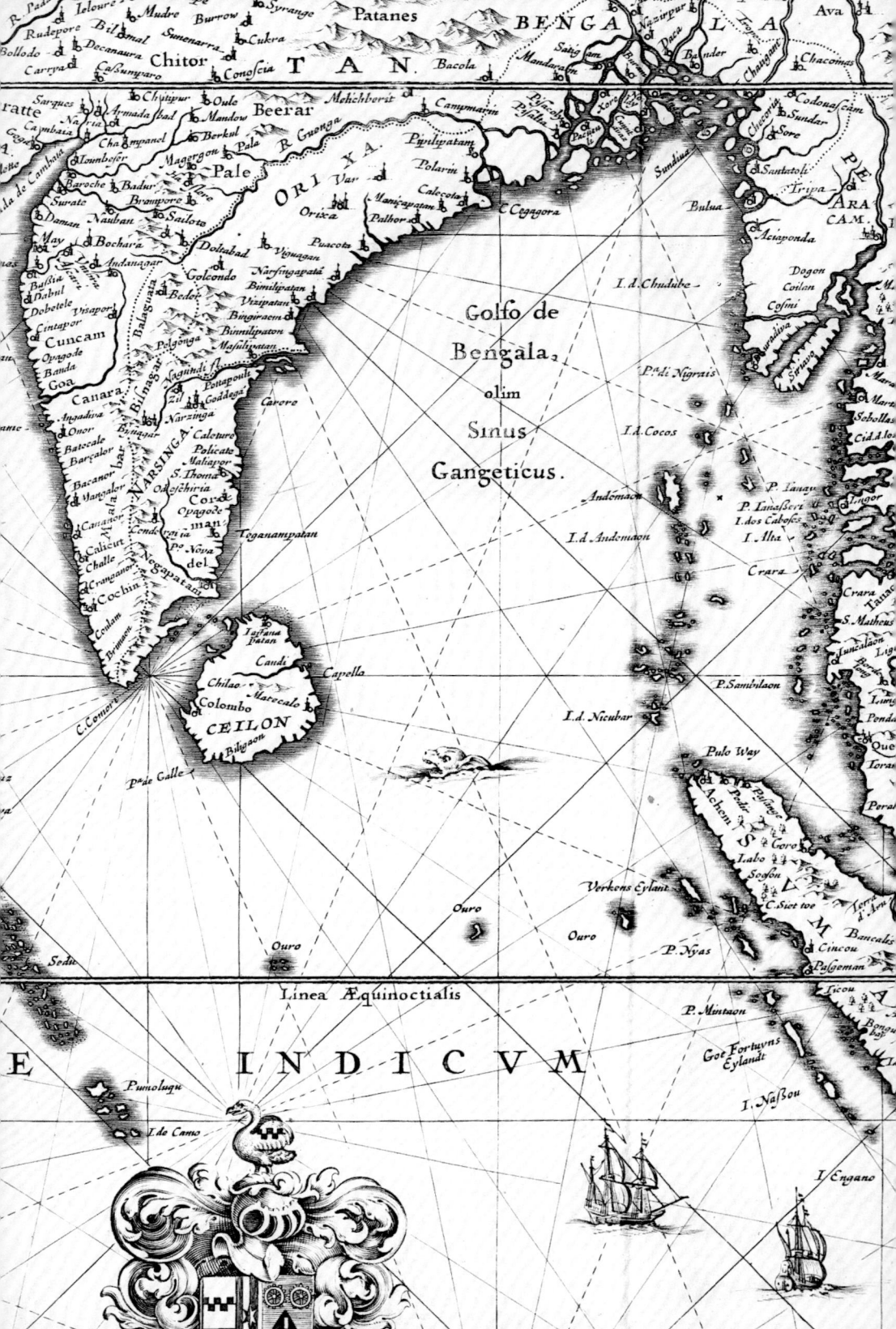

Map of India and the East Indies. The position of Tranquebar is unfortunately not indicated, but the town is situated just north of Negapatam on the east coast of India opposite the northern tip of Ceylon. The map can be dated to 1623. (Frederik V's Atlas, no. 48. The Map Collection, The Royal Library, Copenhagen.)

CHAPTER I
THE BEGINNING

A wave of new enterprise and daring swept over Europe in the first years of the seventeenth century. As early as 1498 the Portuguese had discovered the sea route to India around the southern tip of Africa and had then been able to profit from their monopoly for a hundred years without interference from other European nations. But in 1600 the English formed their East India Company with a patent from Queen Elizabeth I, and in 1602 the Netherlands followed suit with a similar company, the VOC. From then on English and Dutch ships brought their own rich cargoes home.

At this time the East was still something of a fairytale land. It was here all the exotic new spices were to be found; here were pearls and diamonds, peculiar creatures such as elephants, tigers, crocodiles, monkeys, and peacocks. And possibly in some still unknown country – though the likelihood seemed to diminish with every passing year – the strange people spoken of in the Middle Ages: men with dog's heads; men with one foot so large it could be used as a parasol to shield one from the sun; men with such long ears that one could lie on one of them and use the other as a coverlet.

The spices, however, were real enough, although the old stories of how on some islands they lay on the ground in such heaps that they could easily be shovelled into sacks were somewhat exaggerated. In the beginning it had been the spices that had drawn the Europeans out on the dangerous long voyages down the western coast of Africa in the hope of finding a sea route to India, and now that the Portuguese, English, and Dutch companies had established trading stations in the East a steady stream of the costly merchandise flowed around the Cape of Good Hope to Europe.

To be sure, the days were long past when pepper was weighed on special scales behind closed doors for fear that a breath of air might carry away even a grain of the precious condiment. The demand for the eastern spices had grown rapidly: by 1620 annual imports are said to have reached 7,000,000 pounds of pepper, 490,000 pounds of cloves, 450,000 pounds of nutmeg, and 180,000 pounds of mace. But even in Leyel's time, more than a hundred years after Vasco da Gama, prices were still so high that even though ships were regularly lost on the long voyage around Africa the few that came safely home with a reasonable cargo could easily outweigh the loss. Only one of Magellan's five ships reached harbour in Spain after circumnavigating the globe, but its load of cloves was sold with a profit of 2500 per cent.

At this time it was the custom in Europe to boil meat and fish slowly with many spices so as to preserve the food; but it was also a question of giving some taste to the otherwise monotonous and stodgy diet. Meat might be steeped in honey with large amounts of pepper, ginger, and cloves. And sauces, jams, and many kinds of sweets were seasoned with the new condiments. We still make ginger-snaps, and old sources mention ginger-, clove-, and cinnamon sweets served as a special treat at the tables of the rich.

The spices were also mixed in wine. People grew to like spiced wines, such as hippocras, new concoctions that tickled the palate with a tinge of the South.

Lastly, the spices were also used for medicinal purposes. Every apothecary of any note had jars standing on his shelves inscribed "indicum" or "arabicum". Oil of cloves was generally recognized as a remedy for toothache, while both oil of cloves and oil of cinnamon were considered excellent as purifying agents, or as we would say today, disinfectants. About 1575 a Swedish doctor recommended cinnamon and ginger as effective remedies for stomach complaints, coughs, and headaches. Spices were useful as a curative for all sorts of ills; one man even recommended ginger as a component in a very expensive ointment for horses.

Until 1623 the Netherlands had held the supremacy of the Banda Islands, a group of islands south of the Moluccas. This meant that they practically held a monopoly on the nutmeg and mace trade; besides which, most of the cloves came from the small islands of Ternate and Tidore. VOC's headquarters at Batavia on Java soon became a sort of entrepôt for these spices. The Dutch spared no effort in keeping other nations away, even going so far as to fell all clove and nutmeg trees in places where they were unable to control sales.

In 1616 Danish merchants began to speculate on how they might get a share of some of the huge profits to be made out of the East India trade. Two Dutch merchants, Jan de Willum and Herman Rosenkranz, who had settled in Denmark, helped to establish what has been called the first Danish limited company with a twelve-year monopoly on all trade to East India, China, and Japan. However, nothing much happened until a Dutch adventurer, Marcelis de Boshouwer, appeared saying that he came as a delegate from the emperor of Ceylon (now Sri Lanka), offering to give Denmark a monopoly on all trade with the island in return for a little military assistance against his enemies.

Boshouwer succeeded in gaining the interest of King Christian IV, and in 1618 a commercial treaty was signed between the Danish king and the Emperor Adassin. No time was wasted, and in November of that year the new company's first expedition sailed under the command of a young man, Ove Gjedde, who was only twenty-four. However, a fast little ship the *Øresund* was sent in advance of the fleet under the command of yet another Dutchman, the older and more experienced Roland Crappe, so that he might make himself acquainted with conditions in the East and prepare the way for Ove Gjedde.

However, Boshouwer died on the voyage out to Ceylon, and it was soon apparent that his promises of a lucrative trade with the island were as insubstantial as the tropical mists. Instead, Crappe decided to try his luck in India, but his ship was attacked and sunk by the Portuguese off Carical on the eastern coast of India. He himself was rescued and made his way to the local Indian prince, the rajah or nayak of Tanjore (now Thanjavur in Tamil Nadu), whom he may have known from previous visits. And it was here, thanks to Crappe's ingenuity and the prince's goodwill, that the Company obtained a piece of land on the coast around the small village of Tranquebar and the right to build a fortress there, which they called Dansborg, to protect its trade.

In the following years the Danish company sent a number of ships to Tranquebar, but compared with the rich Dutch company the Danish effort was a poor one. Several small vessels were sent out to be used in the local trade along the Indian coast and to the trading stations in Sumatra, Java, and Celebes (now Sulawesi). But a couple of the vessels, the *Jupiter* and the *Nightingale*, were wrecked before the Company derived much benefit from them. Some large ships were also sent out, but the *Flensborg* was attacked and sunk by the Portuguese off the Cape of Good Hope; a man-of-war, the *Pearl*, armed with thirty-two guns, made a successful voyage to Tranquebar, but on the homeward voyage it was very nearly wrecked and only with great difficulty did it manage to creep into an Irish harbour. However, the cargo was safe when the ship finally reached Copenhagen in the summer of 1626; it consisted of a large quantity of pepper and indigo, cotton goods, silks and gold-embroidered textiles. There was also a muslin so fine that it was popularly called "the flying wind", and even some bags of rubies, pearls, and diamonds.

A much smaller ship, the *Christianshavn*, made several voyages to India. On the first, in 1622-24, it brought a large quantity of pepper and a good store of Indian textiles home, but there is no mention of other spices. As early as October 1624 it left on a second voyage, and continued to sail back and forth for several years, though it is impossible to follow its movements in detail. Though the sources do not tell of its departure, it was probably on its way home from yet another voyage in 1635 when as a partial wreck it reached the Irish coast. In the late summer it finally reached Copenhagen with its cargo, which the Company at once had transferred to its brick building by the canal in the centre of Copenhagen, a gift from His Majesty. The cargo consisted of 83,940 pounds of cloves, 73,893 pounds of pepper, 28,142 pounds of saltpetre, 19,050 pounds of white cotton yarn, 17,900 pounds of sapanwood (for the dyeing industry), 6338 pounds of brown sugar, 1617 pounds of rock candy, 1817 pounds of ginger, as well as a store of China root, indigo, rhubarb, porcelain, damask, taffeta, satin, and some diamonds, a cargo purchased in the East for 58,000 rigsdaler, the estimate of its value in Copenhagen being 145,000.

That summer the King wished to know whether the Company had found buyers for the cargo and how far it had got in equipping a new expedition. The letter sheds an amusing light on the King's never failing interest in Company affairs. Before he left Copenhagen he had got one of the councillors to get hold of a list of the various goods on the *Christianshavn* as well as the prices fixed for each commodity. The King had then gone to Glückstadt on the Elbe, at that time a Danish city, and had at once sent to Hamburg and asked his messenger to buy a pound of each article. By this means he discovered that with the exception of the cloves all the goods in Copenhagen were being sold at a far lower price, or at best the same. Thus, a pound of cotton yarn went for 3 daler in Hamburg, but in Copenhagen it only cost one; and the finest loaf sugar was sold in Copenhagen at the ridiculously low price of 16 shillings, while in Hamburg twenty-three were demanded for a much poorer quality. The King was annoyed: "If they go on like this I wonder how they expect to finance a new expedition." He had reason to fear that the Company's directors could cause irreparable damage to the Company's finances, and as he remarked rather drily, they were not so wealthy that they could make good the loss themselves.

A week later he wrote to the treasurers. It was rumoured in Glückstadt that the Company in Copenhagen had sold goods worth 10,000 daler from the cargo to a merchant from Lübeck. But when the King thought of the prices he had seen the Company charge he could by no means accept any such deal – so he commanded that nothing be sold until he himself returned to the capital. He would far rather buy the whole cargo himself and sell it at a fair price since others managed so badly. The Company's deficit was already astronomical and now the directors neglected the chance of recouping some of their losses.

From now on the few ships that returned safely all brought good cargoes of spices. In this period the above-mentioned Dutchman Roland Crappe was governor of Tranquebar, and in spite of the Dutch company's attempts to defend their monopoly he had found means to buy spices on some of the East Indian Islands, especially cloves in Macassar on Celebes. He had already managed to buy pepper on the Malabar coast as a return cargo for Ove Gjedde's ships, and in the ensuing years pepper formed a regular part of every cargo.

Crappe's capable leadership laid the foundations for the Company's activities in the East. It was he who had negotiated with the rajah of Tanjore and been granted Tranquebar and the right to levy taxes there and build a fortress. Without him Ove Gjedde would not have achieved much. When Crappe entered the service of the Danish Company he had already made five voyages to India, the first as a boy and later as a merchant in the VOC. He had an unusual gift for dealing with the Indians, who felt great confidence in him and received him with joy when in 1624 he arrived at Tranquebar while the town was besieged by the rajah's soldiers. They felt that now he was there peace would soon be restored. And he did quickly conclude a peace and restore order to the Company's affairs.

He established factories at Masulipatnam on the east coast of India, and at Pipeley and Balasore in the Ganges delta, in Achin on the northern tip of Sumatra, and at Japara or Bantam on Java, and finally at Macassar on Celebes. In these places he posted reliable men to manage the purchase of local produce, so that a cargo would be ready whenever it was possible to send a ship to collect it. This trade with the various local trading stations was for many years to be the mainstay of the Company's income. The stations might now and then be closed down or re-opened in new places, but the pattern was much the same throughout the entire period.

In 1625 the *Jupiter* anchored with a valuable cargo off the Danish trading station at Balasore. However, the local rajah put the whole crew in prison, and when the ship with no crew on board was cast ashore that night the cargo, according to existing legislation, fell to the rajah. A score of the Danish prisoners died in the prison, and some maintained that they had been poisoned by the rajah. However, it may have been a simple case of food-poisoning. It was a hard blow for the infant Danish Company. Crappe estimated the loss of the ship itself at 20,000 rigsdaler, although it had probably only cost about 2300. But its value in Indian waters, where it was practically irreplaceable, was naturally another matter. The value of the cargo he estimated at 150,000 rigsdaler, and to this must be added the expense of ransoming the few survivors from their imprisonment – all in all a heavy blow to the Company's finances.

In October 1624 the directors of the Company in Copenhagen had succeeded in sending off two more ships: the *Christianshavn*, now on its second voyage to Tranquebar, and a sloop, the *Nightingale*. The fitting out of the two ships cost 97,500 rigsdaler. They arrived in 1625, and soon afterwards Crappe sailed off with them on a local trading voyage, first to Masulipatnam on the east coast of India, which had originally been a small fishing hamlet, but an increasing amount of trade had transformed it into the most important port in the kingdom of Golconda.

The governor here was a distinguished gentleman who lived surrounded by a magnificent court. A large parasol was always carried over him as a token of his authority, and at night his palanquin was surrounded by ten torchbearers.

At this time the city was already an important centre of commerce with many Persian and Arab merchants from whom it was possible to buy the textiles greatly in demand on the Sunda Islands, and on the return of the ships these same merchants would buy their cargoes of cloves, pepper, and nutmeg. Crappe established a Danish station here and then sailed on to Macassar, from where he sailed again in May 1626 with a fine cargo of cloves. He continued to Succedana and Bandjarmasin on southern Borneo, where he established new stations and concluded this stage of his voyage at Bantam on Java.

Bantam was situated in the middle of a fertile area where tons of pepper were grown, but the climate proved to be very unhealthy for Europeans. The English trading station here stood in the middle of a Chinese suburb, which the Europeans described as a stinking puddle of mud. The place was rife with diseases – the two most common being malaria and dysentery. Some thought that dysentery was caused by an excessive indulgence in toddy, others that certain fruits, such as oranges, were dangerous. A number of household remedies were said to be beneficial, such as lemon juice, pomegranates, and cold baths.

During the season the harbour was full of Chinese junks with their huge square sails. Many Chinese merchants had established themselves in the town, so that it had become an entrepôt for goods brought from India through the Sunda Straits instead of through the Straits of Malacca, which were controlled by the Portuguese.

In spite of all Crappe's perseverance and skill the Company was again subject to large financial losses when the *Nightingale* was lost in a hurricane off the coast of Bengal. The ship was wrecked in the heavy surf and the cargo was lost; the crew managed to get ashore, but were kept in prison by the rajah until the Company sent "presents" amounting to 20,000 rigsdaler. Crappe managed to bring the *Christianshavn* safely into Balasore, but found there was little merchandise to be had and was further delayed because of lengthy negotiations with the local rajah before the survivors from the *Nightingale* were released. There was no shortage of problems for him to deal with.

Stengade nos. 72 and 74 in Elsinore. It was here that Willem Leyel grew up. In the middle of the sixteenth century the houses belonged to Willem's great grandfather Sander Leyel, who was both mayor and collector of the Sound Dues. Stengade was formerly paved, hence the name (Stone Street). (Photo: Elsinore Town Museum.)

CHAPTER 2
WILLEM LEYEL

In 1626 a new man arrived in Tranquebar, a man whose name was to be closely connected with the Danish East India Company, both in Denmark and in Tranquebar. His name was Willem Leyel, and for once there is a good deal of source material about his life. In The National Archives there are a large number of his papers, three bundles of letters in several languages, accounts from his years in Tranquebar, and the reports he sent home from his difficult voyage from Denmark to Tranquebar (1639-44), and from his time as governor there (1644-48). Besides these, we also have King Christian IV's letters, in which one can find bits of information that are of value in understanding Leyel's activities.

He was born in Elsinore, around 1593, where his family was well-to-do and highly respected. His maternal great grandfather, Sander Leyel, had already distinguished himself, and not only in Elsinore. King Christian III is said to have valued him highly, and he was often put in charge of various purchases abroad for the King. He also sent the King regular reports of the news he heard from foreign captains and seamen while performing the duties of his office as collector of the Sound Dues, the tax every ship that passed through the narrow Sound between Elsinore and Helsingborg had to pay. The family's wealth and prestige had increased year by year. Even before the Reformation in 1536 Sander Leyel had obtained the brick kiln belonging to the Carmelites, a profitable business, which he later exchanged for four farms. He built himself a fine house in Stengaden – two handsome neighbouring houses with gables fronting on the street and land stretching all the way to the shore. They were solid constructions, for the buildings, nos. 72 and 74, are still there. The King is said to have visited him here and acted as godfather to one of his sons. Besides all this, he owned ships and carried on a lucrative trade with the Scandinavian countries. He owned Borsholm manor, west of the town, as well as a house in Copenhagen and was made mayor of Elsinore in 1536. Under his industrious management everything seemed to blossom. But as is often the case with clever and independent people he was considered arbitrary and difficult. He had all kinds of monetary success but, on the other hand, he and his wife had sorrows enough – they lost ten small children.

Willem Leyel liked to mention the tradition that the family came from Scotland, where it belonged to the nobility. As his coat of arms Sander (short for Alexander) Leyel had chosen a reproduction of the family's Scottish coat of arms with lozenges and lilies in the four fields, but inverted from the original – probably the ancestors from whom he traced his descent were not legitimate. Both Willem Leyel's father and maternal grandfather had been collectors of the Sound Dues and mayors in Elsinore like his great grandfather. His mother's father, Frederik Leyel, left three children, two sons, Alexander and Frederik and a daughter, Ingeborg. On a sandstone plaque on the family house in Stengaden Frederik Leyel had inscribed a Latin verse based on a text from the Book of Job, chapter 19, verses 25-26, which reads in translation: "For I know that my Redeemer liveth, and on the last day I shall rise and in my flesh see God, my Saviour".

Frederik Leyel was royal collector of the Sound Dues for thirty-nine years and mayor of Elsinore for ten years. He died in March 1601, and his widow and children put up a sepulchral tablet over him in St Olai church, where it can still be seen.

It is worth noting how many mayors there were in the Leyel family. Willem's mother, Ingeborg Frederiksdatter Leyel, married Johan Willumsen, who became mayor of Elsinore in 1618, and when he died in 1623 she married Matthias Hansen, yet another mayor, this time in Copenhagen. Matthias Hansen's daughter, Kirsten Madsdatter, had in her youth been Christian IV's mistress and had borne him a son, Christian Ulrik Gyldenløve. Matthias Hansen built himself a fine town house on Amagertorv in 1616, a stately mansion in the Renaissance style copied from the Netherlands. He built it so solidly that he claimed it would last the next 500 years. So far it has managed 400, though perhaps there is not much of the original structure preserved; but the facade is charming (today the building contains the offices of the Royal Porcelain Factory). Matthias Hansen was a respected and wealthy member of the board of directors of the Icelandic Company.

From his marriage to Ingeborg Leyel, Johan Willumsen had several children besides his son Willem, among them three daughters: Anne, who married the mayor of Malmø just across the Sound and inherited her father's house in this city; Kirstine, who married a promising young man, Morten Madsen, who had been tutor to Christian IV's children and was at this time chaplain to the King in the royal palace of Frederiksborg; and finally Dorete, who married Jakob Tømmermand (ship's carpenter) and remained in Elsinore.

The sources do not tell us much of Willem Leyel's early life. The first time we have any reliable information about him he was employed by the VOC in Batavia, but there is nothing to tell us how he got there. Obviously the years in Elsinore must have opened his eyes to the outside world. Many ships came from the great seafaring nations and anchored off the town in order to pay the Sound Dues. A boy who kept his eyes and ears open was bound to be fascinated by the many exciting new place names mentioned by the sailors: the Cape of Good Hope, the gate to all the riches of the East; China, the Moluccas, Sumatra, Surat, Goa, Zanzibar, and across the Atlantic, Cartagena, Mexico, Habana. Now and then a sailor would have had a monkey or a parrot and could tell incredible tales of sea snakes, or a tiger hunt, of cannibals, crocodiles and elephants, of tornadoes and shipwreck.

At this time Elsinore was bubbling with life, and the many ships brought news from all over the world, so that the collectors of the Dues were often more quickly and better informed than anybody else in the whole kingdom. It is suggestive that Henrik Hess, who was for some time the commandant of the fortress of Dansborg, came from Elsinore, where his father was a member of the town council at the same time as Leyel's father was mayor. So it is not unlikely that the two men knew each other, and it may well have been Hess who persuaded Leyel to leave the VOC and take up a position with the Danes at Tranquebar.

In 1618 the Dutch had some fortifications on the island of Onrust off the city of Jakarta (now Djakarta) on Java, and in 1619, after having fought off a naval attack by the English as well as an attack by a Javanese army, they made the city a centre for all their trade in the East under the Dutch name of Batavia. Leyel was about twenty-six at that time and had possibly already been in the service of the Dutch company for some time.

The only piece of evidence that relates (presumably) to his life about this period is a passage by the Dutch scholar Ludovicus de Dieu in the prologue to his edition (1639) of the Persian "Historia Christi", where he writes: "I owe it to the Danish merchant Willem Leyel to confess that the information that this man, raised above the ordinary spirit of commerce, though no scholar, while he still lived in Persia, learned to speak, read, and write the Persian language, passed on to me, when he spent some time in Leyden, has been very useful."

Leyel thus forms an exception to the commonly held image of the men who conducted the business of buying and selling in the distant

Danish possessions, who are usually viewed as sitting with their noses buried in their accounts, longing for the day when they could return home with a large store of gold pieces in the bottom of their chests. Men who evinced no interest whatsoever in the magnificent culture of the East, in its history or literature, if only they could make a good profit.

Several things seem to show that Leyel was an intelligent man with an unusually alert and inquisitive mind. It must have taken some energy to learn to read, write, and speak Persian. However, he need not have lived in Persia in order to have learned Persian. For many years there had been many Persian merchants all over the East, and Persian was the most commonly used language in all commercial dealings among the local peoples. It should also be remembered that during the rule of the Moguls Persian was the administrative language of their entire Indian kingdom and was furthermore a language that conferred great cultural prestige on those who mastered it and had studied its sophisticated literary heritage. Persian was also for many years the language of diplomacy in India. Indeed, as late as the eighteenth century, when the Tranquebar missionary Christian Friedrich Schwartz was granted an audience by the rajah of Tanjore, the two men conversed in Persian.

But if it is true that Leyel spent some time in Persia, it cannot have been for very long. The first Dutch commercial expedition arrived in Persia in June 1623 and succeeded in establishing a trading station. It was especially the Persian silk that interested the European merchants. So it may have been at about this time that Leyel, after having served some years in Batavia, was employed here. All we know about his time in Batavia is that he married a Dutch widow who brought a daughter Christina with her into the family. At least two sons, Hans and Anders, were born to them.

In 1626 we find Leyel, together with a comrade, Claus Rytter, in Pipeley in the Ganges delta, where the Danes had already made a couple of unsuccessful attempts to gain a foothold, and where the Company's ship, the *Nightingale* had been wrecked in a hurricane. Crappe's plan had been to send Erik Grubbe from Pipeley to Delhi to the court of the Great Mogul hoping there to obtain an official permit to trade in his kingdom. But when the *Jupiter* and the *Nightingale* were wrecked so soon after each other the station was left without funds so that they could not afford rich presents worthy of the Mogul. Hence Crappe decided not only to give up the mission to the Mogul, but at least for the present to abandon the trade in Bengal. The stations at Pipeley and Balasore were left in the charge of Indian caretakers, and Leyel and Rytter returned to Tranquebar. Erik Grubbe, who had come out to India together with Ove Gjedde and had deserted in Ceylon when Gjedde sailed home, seems to have spent the remainder of his days in Tranquebar, where he died in 1631. Willem Leyel, on the other hand, probably decided to return home to Denmark.

Many of the leading men in Tranquebar were so angry at the rajah's conduct over the imprisonment and holding to ransom of the crew of the *Nightingale*, that they wanted to declare war on the Bengalis, not on land as the Danes had no army, but at sea where a ship like the *Christianshavn* with its great cannons would be far superior to anything the Indians could construct. By seizing some of the Mogul's ships they could recoup all the great losses they had suffered. However, Crappe urged caution and thought they should wait and see. About this time he bought a small sloop *Posthesten*, which did good service for some years, and possibly also some other Indian vessels.

Times were difficult in most of India. All through Deccan and the Gujarat the monsoon failed in 1630-31, and the rice withered and died in the fields. The cattle could not find grass or feed of any kind, and the country suffered from a terrible famine, which as always was followed by plague. Poor people died by the thousand, and many, as a last resort, sought to sell their children as slaves; a child could be bought for a measure of rice to the value of a small coin worth 5 fanum, and the merchants quickly found that these children could be sold with a large profit in the Sunda Islands. But there were also horrendous stories of people who slaughtered and ate their own children or made away with people who lived alone and were unable to defend themselves.

The famine made it difficult to find the Indian cotton goods that were usually given in exchange for the spices at Macassar and on Java and Borneo, so that the prices rose sharply. But for once Crappe had been fortunate. He happened to have a large stock of these textiles and could therefore reap a generous profit. Among other ventures he was said to have sold a large quantity of linen at Macassar for three times the sum it had cost on the Coromandel Coast, so that he was able to pay off a large part of his debts.

In late November 1634 the rajah Ragnato of Tanjore died and his body, accompanied by his 119 wives, was burned on the funeral pyre. He was succeeded by his son Rambandra, who soon afterwards paid a friendly visit to Dansborg with a large escort. However, Crappe had still not returned from his trip to the East Indies so that it fell to the lot of the commandant Christoph von Wittinghof to receive the rajah and show him around the castle.

At that time the news from home was rather alarming. In spite of the warnings of his advisers King Christian had decided to take part in the Thirty Years' War and in 1626 he lost a battle at Lutter am Barenberg, after which the German troops marched up into the defenceless peninsula of Jutland killing and plundering as they went.

It seems likely that Leyel returned home in the middle of this devastation. On May 1, 1628, he was appointed captain in the royal Danish navy with an annual salary of 200 rigsdaler. He undoubtedly carried letters from Crappe both to the King and to the Company directors. He could tell them that the Company now had five trading stations besides Tranquebar. The two most important were those in Masulipatnam and Macassar; but Crappe expressed his conviction that the one at Bantam on Java would also prove valuable, while he was more doubtful about the two on Borneo.

After a peace had been concluded in 1629 the King was again able to take an interest in the Company's affairs. It was decided to dispatch two ships, the man-of-war *Flensborg* and a two-masted sloop. In order to obtain enough capital to equip the vessels it was agreed that all shareholders must pay in a further sum of 20 per cent of their original contribution. Realizing that many would not wish to risk more money the directors decided that if the shareholders did not pay, their former investment would be confiscated. But even this high-handed measure failed to bring in the necessary funds. In consequence the King had to save the financial situation and paid in a considerable sum, so much in fact that he was now designated as the "Head and Lord of the whole Company", and it now became his privilege to nominate the Company's directors.

On the whole it is evident that the shareholders' investments in the Company not only did not give the expected profit, but even their capital investment was lost. Only some of the big merchants who made a profit by fitting out the expeditions and selling the goods brought home from the East caught a glimpse of the huge returns originally promised the shareholders.

The two ships sailed in late 1629 and were shortly followed by a two-masted vessel, the *Fortuna*. But the Company was still dogged by ill-luck. Off the Cape of Good Hope the magnificent ship *Flensborg* got into a fight with some Portuguese ships who were trying to maintain the monopoly on all trade with India which they claimed had been given to them by the Pope. Unfortunately the *Flensborg* caught fire and blew up. Most of the men on board were killed, only forty-two being taken prisoner. However, two smaller ships managed to reach Tranquebar, but one of them, *Falken*, only after a very difficult passage that cost the lives of most of the crew.

In spite of the lengthy interruption in all correspondence with Denmark Crappe proved to be equal to the challenge. If he could not obtain powder from home he would have to manufacture it himself. All the ingredients were available. Coal and sulphur were in plentiful supply, and an excellent quality of saltpetre could be obtained from the Sunda Islands. In the same way they would have to make their own rope for the ships, but rope could easily be spun from coconut fibres just as the Indians had done for centuries. Finally he established a smithy to make all kinds of equipment for the ships – they had difficulty making the big anchors, but otherwise the smiths could produce most of the necessary ironwork.

He also had to reorganize the trade. If no money or goods arrived from home the economy had to be based on trade with the stations around the Indian Ocean where Crappe now seems to have concentrated on Masulipatnam, Macassar, and Bantam. In 1631 Copenhagen managed to send out another sloop, the *Charitas*; but though it reached India without difficulty it brought few fresh supplies in the way of men or money, and Crappe still had only the small sloops at his disposal, while both the Dutch and the English had much larger ships and despised his efforts. The Dutch loved to tell how Crappe owed so much money in Masulipatnam that he no longer dared to put into the harbour there. If this is true it seems to have been only a temporary embarrassment for in 1634 the *Charitas* called here and unloaded fifty-three bars of cloves, as well as sandalwood, turtleshell, silk, and porcelain.

When the news of the disaster of the *Flensborg* reached Copenhagen it led to speculation as to whether the King and the Company would be able to invest more capital in the East Indian trade. It was clearly a losing concern. Some of the directors claimed that it would be best to abandon the whole venture, sell Dansborg and the trifling amount of goods still left in the warehouses to the Dutch company and recall the men – and admit that the whole venture had been a failure. The Danes had simply found the task beyond their powers and would now be the laughing stock of all their competitors.

Others maintained that they should wait and see. The Company had been overtaken by a number of disasters, but this could hardly continue. Their fortunes might change. A good foundation had been laid; Roland Crappe was a clever and wholly trustworthy leader – things would almost surely get better.

The sources do not tell us what Willem Leyel did in the years after 1628 when, as mentioned above, he was at home in Denmark and had been made a captain in the Danish navy. But we can see that in January 1634 he was summoned to former admiral Albret Skeel at the navy base Bremerholm in Copenhagen. The conversation turned on the wretched state of the Company's finances. It owed the royal treasury the enormous sum of 156,000 rigsdaler, and the question was whether it was worthwhile to keep on pouring money into its seemingly bottomless coffers. It was obvious that one of the reasons for the small returns was that the Danish Company's investments were very small compared with its competitors. One had only to compare one of the largest ships the Company had managed to send out during these years, i.e. the *Pearl*, which was of 900 tons burden and armed with thirty-two guns, with one of the huge Portuguese carracks of 1500 tons. And as early as the end of the sixteenth century the Dutch had sent out sixty-five ships to the East in only six years, while the Danish Company often could not manage even a single ship a year, and most of these were small sloops. So, all things considered, it was not surprising that the Company did not reap the huge returns its competitors received.

Skeel could tell how the King had written to him, asking him to consider what could be done; he was to apply both to the vice-chancellor and the professors at the University and also ask the opinion of the ordinary shareholders and then send some representatives of these people to a meeting on March 10 at Skanderborg Castle in Jutland. But prior to this the King wished to have an opportunity to discuss the whole matter with Leyel, because Leyel had returned from India a short while ago and thus must be the man who knew most about conditions there.

This last bit of information is of interest, because no other source suggests that Leyel had recently returned from India – as far as we know he had been in Denmark since 1628. Perhaps the reasoning was that six years could not make so much difference. Perhaps he had made a voyage in one of the Company ships of which we have no trace. There is no way of knowing.

In the above-mentioned letter to Albret Skeel the King writes that he realizes that the Company lacks both men and ships, "because on the first of the two latest expeditions one vessel was lost with its crew and everything, and the other sloop also lost most of its crew near Caput Bonae Spei (the Cape of Good Hope) and only reached India after suffering great hardships". This first expedition must refer to the loss of the *Flensborg* and the *Fortuna*'s difficult passage.

There is no reason to doubt that Christian IV with his usual energy had made himself master of every detail of the Company's business. When Leyel arrived at Skanderborg and was called in to the King the latter pointed out that the latest reports on the Company's situation were very discouraging; but, on the other hand, he felt it would be discreditable for him to give up or sell Dansborg to a foreign nation – that was not what he had had in mind when he had spent so much money to establish the Company and had sent ships to the East. So, on the whole, he thought it better to run some risk in trying to save what was left than to give up and so lose everything.

Leyel probably agreed with the King, and the latter seems then to have asked him to go out once more, now as merchant-in-chief, as he, with his experience, would have the best chance of succeeding in restoring the Company's finances in India.

In his letter to Albret Skeel the King had offered to equip a new vessel and do his best either to equip a sloop himself or persuade others to do so and then hand both over to the Company for a new venture. But it had been estimated that it would take at least 600,000 rigsdaler in ready money and goods, a sum that might well make one pause and reflect before proceeding.

In his meeting with the shareholders the King repeated his promise to lend the Company a ship and equip it; but he felt that if he did this others ought to furnish a sloop as an accompanying vessel.

Leyel must have enjoyed the full confidence of the King, for he returned to Copenhagen with a letter with a royal command to admiral Klaus Daa to give Leyel an opportunity to inspect the King's 630 ton ship *St Anna* to see if it was suitable, and if Leyel found it unsuitable the admiral was to be so good as to show him another. The two men were also to find a small merchant sloop of 200 or 240 tons to accompany the larger ship. Leyel approved the *St Anna*, and he now became the backbone of the new venture as the merchant with the responsibility for buying new goods and equipment.

Later that summer he received another 200 rigsdaler to make a trip to the Netherlands in the King's service. Nothing is said as to the exact purpose of his trip, but there can be little doubt that he used the opportunity to make a careful study of the VOC's goods and prices.

Chapter 3
PREPARATIONS FOR THE VOYAGE

When Leyel returned he found that it had been decided that the *St Anna* would sail for the East as soon as she was ready. As an accompanying vessel the directors had chosen the 234 ton sloop *St Jakob*. As early as February the King had written to the treasurers in Copenhagen with orders for them to lay aside all the canvas woven in the state prison for use in the *St Anna*. Another letter from the King commanded that the *St Jakob* should be sheathed with copper to protect the wooden planks from the dreaded ship worm (*teredo navalis*) that infests tropical waters. In a short time the worms can render the planks so flimsy that one can stick a finger through them.

Leyel now had a busy time procuring trading goods for the ship. Among other things he spent 4000 rigsdaler for lead, always a commodity that was much in demand in the East, 4000 rigsdaler for quicksilver, bought vermillion for another 4000, amber for 400 rigsdaler, and alum (a white salt used in dyeing) for 800 rigsdaler. The King had also ordered twenty-two casks (14,450 litres) of wine, two casks (1313 litres) of brandy, and eight casks (5255 litres) of vinegar, the money to be taken from the customs income, and he had also promised to provide the two ships with victuals and all other necessaries. Nobody could accuse him of being miserly!

On the other hand, King Christian was always careful in money matters. The admiral Klaus Daa and the treasurers were ordered to see that the money and supplies delivered to Willem Leyel were used solely for fitting out the *St Anna*. At the same time the King asks for information as to "how the money given to Willem Leyel for fitting out the 'St Anna' is being spent".

In the meantime work was going on at full speed in the Naval Yard to fit out the ships for the voyage. But things seemed to move slowly, and this did not please the King. On November 11 he wrote to the treasurers that they "should remind the chief of the Naval Yard Erik Ottesen Orning and the master of Bremerholm Rasmus Sørensen Samsing that they are to make all possible speed to finish work on the *St Anna* as soon as may be and keep the King informed". The King kept an eye on the matter: when the work seemed to drag the two gentlemen got a reminder sent from Flensborg in early December.

St Anna was to have a crew of 140, and the round trip to India was calculated to take two and a half years. The victuals loaded were 70,000 pounds of ship's biscuits, 30,000 pounds of salt beef, 6000 pounds of salt pork, 8000 pounds of dried cod, 750 cheeses of 50-60 kilos each, 52,556 litres of water, 15,766 litres of French wine, 30,219 litres of Spanish wine, 29 casks of butter, besides brandy, vinegar, lemon juice, prunes, barley, beans, peas, hams, smoked and salt ox-tongues, and horseradish.

The lemon juice is interesting, for it seems to show that Leyel was aware of the great benefit of the juice in preventing scurvy. This dreadful illness at this time practically always accompanied ships as a horrible stowaway on lengthy voyages, and caused innumerable deaths. Leyel may possibly have heard of the Englishman James Lancaster, who in the year 1600 sailed to the East with a number of ships from the English East India Company and wrote that he had given his men three spoonfuls of lemon juice first thing every morning by which means he had cured many sailors and preserved the rest from scurvy.

The winter of 1634-35 was very severe. The Øresund froze over. This may have been the reason why it took so long to get the *St Anna* ready. And worse was to follow when, in February 1635, a messenger came with the news that the *Christianshavn*, which had been said to be on its way home from the East and had been almost despaired of, had finally arrived at Youghal in Ireland. Many of the crew had died and the ship was a partial wreck; but a good load of pepper, cloves, sugar, and cotton was fairly intact. So the King gave orders that the necessary equipment be taken from the *St Anna*, "as it won't be able to sail before October", and sent to Ireland with the warship *Tre Løver* (three lions – a symbol from the Danish coat-of-arms), as soon as the ice broke up. He also commanded that 1000 rigsdaler be sent to the men on the *Christianshavn*; the wealthy merchant Johan Braëm was to furnish the money against security in the cargo. The King maintained that the latter could probably afford to wait for his money, the poor men on board could not. Christian IV felt a real concern for the sailors.

The Company had thus been forced to give up any hope of sending the *St Anna* off for the time being. The King even had plans of selling the ship to the Portuguese. Instead, every effort was made to get the *St Jakob* off. With his usual attention to detail King Christian wrote to the treasurers that they were to let the Company take what was needed to fit out the sloop for the voyage to India, and they could take wine and victuals from the stores laid in for the *St Anna*, but they had to give an undertaking that the Company would repay everything before Michael-mas.

Towards the end of February Leyel had again been with the King, this time in Koldinghus castle. This can be seen from a royal letter of February 27, 1635, to the treasurers regarding an oven; it bears the superscription "cette lettre avec Villom Leyel", another indication of how much the King relied on Leyel's first-hand knowledge of conditions in the East.

It was probably at this meeting that the King sounded Leyel out as to the possibility of trading with Surat, the important Indian commercial centre on the northwestern coast of India, where both the English and the Dutch had established trading stations. And what about the other countries belonging to the Mogul? Or Persia, where both of these na-tions were trying to get a share in the silk trade? The King knew that Leyel had been in these districts and probably knew more about them than any other Dane. Duke Friederich III of Gottorp was also known to have plans to send ambassadors through Russia to the Persian Shah in Isfahan to negotiate a trade agreement in order to realize his dream of making Friedrichstadt on the Ejder a centre of all Northern European trade in silk. King Christian could not stand by while a competitor made off with all the profits – if there were any. For the King distrusted the whole idea: "These people who plan to establish trade with Persia have promised the grand duke in Moscow that they will immediately pay in a capital of six times 100,000 Daler to finance the trade. It would be nice to know where that money is to come from".

Leyel was asked to send a summary of everything he had told the King to the Chancellor, Christian Friis. This resulted in a long letter dated February 22, 1635, from Kolding, in which Leyel points out that other nations are trading in these places, "and this trade is of great importance for us as soon as we have stabilized our trading stations in Bantam and Jamby on account of a number of goods that are to be had in Persia and the lands belonging to the Mogul and can be sold with great profit in Bantam, Jamby, and Macassar as also here in our own country; in like manner it would be possible to sell goods we can purchase in our own trading stations with a large profit in Persia and in the Mogul's lands, so that one region can always make the other very profitable for us".

Leyel also related how Roland Crappe as early as 1626 had had similar plans, and that as mentioned above he had sent Erik Grubbe, Claus Ryt-ter and himself to Bengal to obtain money for travelling expenses and presents for the Great Mogul. According to his plan Grubbe was to have asked the Mogul for trading rights in his lands in the same way as the Mogul had made such agreements with other European countries. But due to the many disasters that had overtaken the Company in Bengal at this time Grubbe had found it impossible to raise the necessary funds so that he had had to abandon the whole idea.

So Leyel now proposed that the Company, with the next ships to the East Indies, send out "an experienced and suitable person" with letters from the King to the countries in question to ask for trading rights and if possible freedom from duties. It would be best if such a person began his journey somewhere on the Coast of Coromandel and from there went first to the kingdom of Golconda to negotiate with the rajah there, then on to the Mogul in Delhi, and finally to the Shah in Persia, and from there began his journey home. One cannot help feeling that Leyel was eager to make the journey himself – he was probably one of the few men suitable for the venture.

Roland Crappe had now served the Company faithfully ever since he had sailed out in advance of Ove Gjedde's ships with the *Øresund* in 1618. Leyel and the others always mentioned him with respect, and felt that Crappe had an unusual understanding of trade in the East Indies and a unique ability to deal with the various rajahs and officials by which means he had procured many advantages for the Company. To be sure, there were those on the board of directors who criticized him for using too much money on presents for such men. But Leyel maintained that such money was well spent, and that the gentlemen at home probably found it difficult to understand the way things were done in the East. Out there it was an established fact that little could be achieved without giving generous presents.

Late in April it was announced that, as a reward for his having served the King as a petty officer for twelve years and having filled the difficult post as general and governor of Dansborg for another twelve, Crappe was to be knighted and given a coat of arms – this was to be "an Indian on a white shield dressed according to the custom of that country with a red band around his head and a white skirt, with his musket in his hand, and an Indian of similar appearance on the helmet between the two horns, each being half red and half white". Furthermore, Crappe now decided to call himself Crappé – it sounded French and aristocratic.

In the late summer the *Christianshavn* finally arrived in Copenhagen from Ireland with its cargo, which the Company now busily unloaded and stored in the stone building on the street "Ved Stranden", on the banks of the canal opposite Christiansborg, given to them by the King. The Company's accounts were not good, indeed, they had been so much in the red for the last score years that the officials feared they had lost all their investments and sent a petition to the King asking him to see that "this venture does not bring more people to absolute poverty than it already has done". Even the King himself, who was in desperate need of cash, must have sighed at the thought of the considerable capital amounting to 173,900 rigsdaler he had invested in the Company with a diminishing hope of ever seeing any of that money again.

The sale of the *St Anna* to the Portuguese was apparently never realized, and in August preparations were made to send both that ship and the *St Jakob* off as soon as possible. Klaus Daa received instructions to begin to recruit enough men for the crews.

In September the King came himself to Kronborg to count the money in the great chest in the Sound Duty's office. There proved to be quite a large sum. In rigsdaler and rose-nobles it amounted to 15,500 daler, which he now laid in another chest, where "the money is to remain until it please God that the 'St Anna' puts to sea". Besides this sum the King had 20,000 daler deposited with the commissariat in Skåne, and in the keeping of Jonas Heinemark, the customs manager in Copenhagen another 12,000, so that he had in all 47,500 rigsdaler for fitting out the ships.

It is impressive that Christian continued to invest so much money in the Company, for both his own and the country's finances were in a desperate state. Many of the lands belonging to the crown were heavily mortgaged, and the King scarcely knew how to find the means to pay the interest at the so-called Kieler-Umschlag, where he had borrowed heavily. Rigsrådet, the council of nobles, owed him large sums, which could not be recovered, and all this meant that neither the members of the court nor the crews in the Navy could be paid. In a curious letter dated December 15, 1635, the King puts forward his personal claim to the money in the Sound Dues chest "for otherwise I have no means to preserve my State". There seems to have been some difficulty in getting the money, so the King employs a stratagem: "Let the Customs officials at Elsinore secretly fill some casks with stones and let Jørgen Vind (the treasurer) take them together with the other coins so that Hans Bøjesen (the royal paymaster) does not notice it".

However, he seems not wholly to have abandoned the belief that the trade with India could restore his hopeless financial circumstances – if only he did not give up.

In the meantime the treasurers had been commanded to deliver to Leyel all the goods he had already ordered, as well as those he might still order in return for a receipt. Still another indication of how highly the King regarded Leyel and trusted his knowledge of the East Indian trade can be seen from the fact that on September 14, 1635 he gave him full powers to act on his behalf in the East India Company at an annual salary of 300 rigsdaler to be paid him by the Company. He is enjoined to watch over the best interests of the King and the Company in accordance with the oath he has sworn.

As the time approached when the *St Anna* and *St Jakob* were to sail the King wrote a letter to the king of Bantam, partly because the latter had sent costly gifts to Christian, and partly because he had permitted Roland Crappé and other Danes to trade in his country. So King Christian wrote a letter of thanks and sent as a gift "a poor thing manufactured in the King's country".

The ships were now practically ready to sail. The crew were busy with the final preparations. On November 6, 1635, the King issued a pass for the *St Anna* to sail to India with Christian Klausen as captain, and on November 19 the two ships finally set sail. Roland Crappé was on board the *St Anna* – he sailed out one last time to set things in order out there and brief his successor about the work. Leyel was chief merchant on board, and Niels Andersen from the small village of Udbyneder (hence he was normally called Niels Andersen Udbyneder) to the south of Mariager Fjord in Jutland was chaplain. On board the *St Jakob* was Berent Pessart, who had been appointed to take over the leadership of the Company in the East when Crappé sailed home. Like both Crappé and Leyel, Pessart had been employed in the service of the Dutch East India Company. He had served that company for several years in Batavia, where he is mentioned in 1631 as a free citizen with a share in a merchant vessel sailing to Cambodia. The *St Anna* and the *St Jakob* carried goods to the value of 17,000 rigsdaler, as well as 33,000 rigsdaler in ready money; a considerable assistance for the financially unsound colony.

The ships reached Tranquebar in safety. Crappé had much to do, arranging the Company's affairs and procuring a return cargo for the *St Anna*. But it was decided that the *St Jakob* should remain in India for use in the trade between the islands. It was at this time that Crappé received an invitation from some local merchants to resume trade in Bengal, promising him a firman (licence) from the Mogul Shah Jahan. For many years almost all trade in India had been in the hands of the Muslims, first and foremost the Arabs and Persians, whom the Europeans called Moors. They had sailed for centuries in these waters and some of their ships were of a considerable size, the largest about 600 tons.

Now Crappé again sent ships to Pipeley and established a profitable trade by a judicious mixture of presents for the top officials and a conspicuous arming of the vessels. The Company's main office was moved from Tranquebar to Masulipatnam, the natural centre for trade along the coast, and here on November 9, 1636, Crappé officially put Berent Pessart in charge of the Company's affairs. A reliable elderly Dutchman Jacob van Stackenborg was to govern in Tranquebar.

Crappé apparently had no difficulty in procuring a good load, especially of cloves, for his return voyage. It is interesting to note that cloves now take a dominant place among the goods bought to send home. The price in India, or perhaps rather in Macassar, is said to have been 76,000 rigsdaler. As there is no information as to the sales price in Denmark, nothing can be said as to any profit, but it was probably excellent. Crappé and Willem Leyel left Tranquebar on January 16, 1637. The voyage home on board the *St Anna* went smoothly and on November 4 that year the ship arrived back in Copenhagen.

CHAPTER 4
THE NEW VOYAGE

In spite of the *St Anna*'s return to Copenhagen with a valuable cargo the Company's financial situation was far from satisfactory. The shareholders had never received any profit on their investment and must by now have thought it hopeless to expect any. The wish to invest more money in the venture was minimal. It was only the King's indomitable will that kept the Company going.

Roland Crappé had been knighted and become a wealthy man, and was probably now middle-aged. The voyage to India with the *St Anna* was his last; but he still lived a number of years in Copenhagen where he bought the Company's large stone house on the banks of the canal opposite Christiansborg.

Time was to show that it was Willem Leyel who took over the leadership of the Company after Crappé. There is, however, a riddle from about this period that seems difficult to resolve if one wishes to form a picture of his career. As stated above he was entrusted with the responsible position of chief merchant on board the *St Anna* and must thus have sailed from Copenhagen on November 19, 1635. This is further confirmed by a letter Leyel wrote to the King's son-in-law Hannibal Sehested in November 1640 when they were both in Madrid. He says here that it had then been his intention with his ship *Christianshavn* to call at Madeira, where he from his own experience knew that he would find a good reception, as he and his crew "da selbst gute Tractement haben empfangen, in Sondernheit in Jahre 1636, das Schiff Sct. Anna". Accordingly, Leyel must have sailed with Crappé in 1635 and have returned with the same vessel in early November 1637.

So far so good. But there exist letters from Christian IV that do not agree with this. On March 11, 1636, the King writes to two prominent merchants in Copenhagen, Jørgen Danielsen and Hans Tregaard: "As the King owns half the shares in the East India Company he has entrusted Willem Leyel to be director and agent on behalf of the King in all Company affairs, and he has taken his oath before the King". He also wrote to the chancellery that Willem Leyel on this day, March 11, 1636, has in the city of Kolding been sworn in before the Chancellor Mr Christian

Friis, Vincent Bilde of Nes and Ove Juel of Meilgaard as director and agent for the East India Company.

The oath he took goes as follows: "He promises and undertakes to serve the King truly and faithfully, to work for the advantage of the King and the shareholders in the East India Company and do his utmost to prevent all harm to them. He must not reveal anything to anybody about the state of the trade to the detriment of the Company. When selling the Company's goods and when buying equipment he must not favour any person, but seek the advantage of the Company, nor must he take part in any of its purchases, sales or contracts, unless it be with the knowledge of the shareholders, and whatever he may learn thereby to the disadvantage of the Company he must pass on, and otherwise in every way conduct himself as an honest and loyal agent should do."

In yet another letter dated November 4, 1636, the King writes to the agents of the East India Company: "Lastly, the King grants that Jahim Pedersen, who has served the Company for some time, may be appointed director. He is to live in Copenhagen and direct the trade jointly with them and Villom Leyel. He is to have the same salary as Villom Leyel."

Three letters that only make sense if Leyel did not sail on board the *St Anna*, but in precisely these years filled a responsible position in Copenhagen. He can hardly have been in two places at once. Perhaps these last facts pertain to another Willem Leyel, an uncle, cousin, or relation of some kind. And perhaps it was this other Willem Leyel who in June 1639 was appointed director in the Company? We are left with a number of unanswered questions.

In the Naval Yard work was already going ahead to outfit a new expedition. It had been decided to send the *Christianshavn* out again – it had already completed the voyage a number of times. The vessel did finally set out in early 1637 under a Captain Tyge Christensen, and the King furnished him with a letter to Roland Crappé asking the latter to assist him according to his instructions if Crappé was still in India. But for some reason the ship had to return, and in May 1638 the King wrote to Corfitz Ulfeldt, who at this time was governor of Copenhagen and had recently married the King's daughter Leonora Christina, that he thought it best if both the *Christianshavn* and another ship which should have been to Japan now sail out together. To save money Ulfeldt is to see to it that the directors lay off the crew on the *Christianshavn* until the ship is again ready to sail – when that time comes "those who are suitable can apply again".

Soon after the *St Anna*'s return Corfitz Ulfeldt is ordered to negotiate with Roland Crappé and try to persuade him to settle permanently in Copenhagen, agree to become Surveyor General of Navy Stores and top director of the Company, and to assume the management of the East India trade. And if Crappé should wish to go out to India again he should give the King timely warning.

Lastly, Ulfeldt is to sell the big house in the street "Ved Stranden" which the King had given to the Company and which had for a long time been the Company's headquarters, and use the money to fit out the ships. As already mentioned Roland Crappé bought the house. Furthermore, the King's son, Christian Ulrik Gyldenløve, wished to resign from his post as president of the Company, and the King suggests that the merchant Johan Braëm take his place.

Crappé immediately got down to work and submitted an estimate of the Company's financial status, in which he writes that if next spring they use 20 per cent of the money from the sale of the *St Anna*'s cargo to fit out a new expedition to India the Company's trade will be so firmly established that a ship can return every year with a good cargo. He apparently had a very optimistic view of the future now that the trade had finally taken a favourable turn.

After the return of the *Christianshavn* from its abortive voyage it was decided to give up sending a ship in 1638, and instead concentrate on finding money for a new expedition. It was not easy. Of the seventeen ships that had been sent out through the years some had been lost, only seven had returned home while others stayed to serve in the local trade. There may of course have been more ships than we know about today; but the proportion is clear. It had been and continued to be a losing concern.

On September 4, letters were sent to the mayors and council in Copenhagen that they must see to it that the Company shareholders pay in the promised 15-20 per cent of their former investment before September 21 with the usual threat that if they fail to do so their former investment will be confiscated. But this produced far too little capital, and the King had once again to make up the deficit. He writes in his diary for March 31, 1639: "I lent the East India Company 10,000 thaler and to those who furnish the powder 4,000 thaler".

However, it was slow work getting the ship off. On February 17 the King writes from Copenhagen Castle to the treasurers asking them for their views on how to get the means to expedite the ship's departure.

In the King's own opinion it must be sufficient if the Company is given a quantity of lead worth 10,000 daler, and it should be ordered so that those who supply the lead receive half the sum now, and the remainder when the ship leaves. One can sense an understandable irritation towards the end of the letter: "I cannot imagine how it can be that the same ship a short while ago was fully equipped and was at sea on its way to East India and now seems to lack everything."

A similar impatient sigh may be seen in a letter from Frederiksborg Castle, where he writes that the money for the directors is now being sent. "God grant that it may be better spent than the former sum."

It was about this time that an Indian elephant arrived in Copenhagen. It is a mystery how it can have got there – there is nothing to show that a Company ship should have arrived about 1639, so it may possibly have come with the *St Anna* in 1637. But no doubt the people of Copenhagen flocked to see the strange animal.

On June 20, 1639, four directors of the East India Company were appointed. The first two were Roland Crappé and Jakob Mikkelsen, who was mayor and in charge of Royal Customs in Copenhagen – he had also invested in several trading companies and was one of the prominent figures in the city. The third appointment went to Johan Braëm, the big merchant, who had reaped large profits, especially from whaling, as director of the Northland Company. And, finally, as no. 4, Willem Leyel. All four were to have a salary of 500 rigsdaler a year – a considerable sum compared to the 200 an ordinary ship's captain received.

This time the Company decided to send out another ship together with the *Christianshavn* and found a fairly large ship *Den forgyldte Sol* (*The Gilded Sun*) of 720 tons, which Christian IV bought for 10,000 speciedaler (a new coin, issued in 1629: 1 speciedaler = 2 rigsdaler). Fitting out the two ships cost 110,000 rigsdaler.

There is no knowing what had happened to *Christianshavn*'s former captain Tyge Christensen – he seems simply to have disappeared after the abortive voyage. It was not easy to find anybody with sufficient experience to replace him, and presumably the Company then put pressure on Willem Leyel. He had formerly been a captain in the King's service, had made the voyage to India several times, and was familiar with the trade out there. Besides, there were disturbing reports as to Berent Pessart's activities in India, and he was not fulfilling his obligation to send regular reports home. Hence it would be expedient to send an experienced man out to report on the situation and take whatever action was necessary.

Leyel accepted the task, but arranged that his old companion from Pipeley, Claus Rytter, was given command of *The Gilded Sun*. Their instructions were that when they reached India the two men were to alternate with Berent Pessart as directors of the Company, each of them presiding over the Council a month at a time – a hopeless arrangement. But Leyel and Rytter could relieve Pessart of his command if they found him incompetent. Leyel seems to have had this last instruction in a sealed envelope, which was not to be opened until Pessart had demonstrated his incompetence. But Leyel had probably been informed as to the contents of the letter.

The two men now hastened to prepare their vessels and cargoes for sea. We still have the muster roll for the *Christianshavn* which shows which men ran away from which harbour, were dismissed or died in service.

As commander of the expedition Leyel was responsible for the diplomatic and commercial problems, whereas the captain of the ship was responsible for the running of the ship. On board the *Christianshavn* the captain was an excellent seaman from the town of Ribe in Jutland called Jørgen Hansen Riber. There was also both a chief mate, Carsten Ludvigsen, and a mate, presumably a Dutchman, Peter de Siwart. Surprisingly there was no chief merchant, possibly Leyel himself filled this position, but there were two merchant's mates: two Dutchmen, Philip de Goltz and Peter Lützen, the latter of whom kept the accounts. And there were five assistants, whose job it was to keep an eye on the merchandise, as well as the ship's stores of victuals, equipment, arms, and ammunition. The ship's chaplain was Lauritz Caspersen.

Once at sea the responsibility for the crew lay with the chief boatswain, Amund Olufsen. The victuals were the responsibility of the steward; and there was both a cook and cook's mate, quartermasters, the barber who also did duty as ship's surgeon, the carpenters and sailmakers, the cooper and the smith, while the provost marshal carried out the punishments served out by the council.

As stated above, aboard the *Christianshavn* it was the merchant's mate, Peter Lützen, who kept the accounts, which have likewise been preserved. At the top of the first page we read: "Laus Deo – Anno 1639 – aboard the ship 'Christianshavn'. In the name of the Holy Trinity. Amen." They were setting out on a dangerous venture, so it was well to have Our Lord with them. The account continues: "Oct. 29: Paid to His Royal Majesty's East India paymasters – 24,000 rigsdaler."

The muster roll from the *Christianshavn*'s voyage and stay in Tranquebar. It begins with the date October 29, 1639, next to which can be read "Cook Hans Søffrenssen died onboard the ship in the Sound", and ends with the death of the boatswain Niels Warbierg in Tranquebar on August 10, 1647. Leyel must have been relieved of his command shortly afterwards. It is worth noting that twenty-two of the thirty men on this first page of the roll absconded. It was difficult to keep the crews together.

As the days passed new expenses were steadily added: large gilt mirrors for use as presents to the Indian princes, boatswain's chests for the crew, slops, and other equipment: 40 pairs of shoes, 30 linen shirts, 50 pairs of Icelandic stockings and 50 pairs of Icelandic gloves, 3 hand axes and 12 Dutch knives, 5½ pounds of brass wire, 2 dozen wooden whistles, 2 pincers, 1 hammer, 2 tinderboxes, 29 packets of small pins, 1000 needles, 3 dozen thimbles, 1 pound tailor's thread, etc.

Besides the crew there were a number of soldiers on board under their corporal, the military force promised to the Ceylonese emperor to help fight against his enemies. At last, on a day in late October they sailed. An Icelander, Jon Olafsson, who took part in the expedition of 1622-24 has left us a detailed description of the *Christianshavn*'s first departure in October 1622, a festive occasion when the King himself, the leading men of the Company, the city mayors and a number of nobles and citizens gathered at the Company's big house to wish the crew Godspeed and a prosperous voyage. The ships lay anchored in the road, probably suitably dressed with flags and pennants. When all were present the head clerk began to read out the names of the crew. This was followed by reading aloud the ship's articles laid down by Christian IV, the rules governing life on board that must be familiar to everybody – be they captain or ship's boy. These articles were usually read aloud at intervals when the ship was at sea to refresh the memory of the sailors. So perhaps it is only right to quote a few of them (these from 1639):

1) First of all, our soldiers and sailors shall swear to serve Us and Denmark faithfully, and with unswerving loyalty to obey the following articles.

23) He that introduces dice, cards, or any other instrument of gaming into the ships or makes such things, shall forfeit a month's wages and spend eight days in irons on bread and water.

27) When the trumpet sounds and the drums are beaten every man shall at once stand to arms in his quarter.

30) He that neglects his watch or lets others take his watch, unless it be done with the consent and knowledge of the commander, shall be punished by death, keelhauling, being tied to the mast, and lose his wages as may be decided by the ship's council.

41) If any man gets drunk he shall each time be punished by the loss of a month's wages and further punishment as the circumstances warrant.

44) Nobody – of whatever rank, whether officer or crew member – shall dare to bring or use tobacco on board, the penalty being the loss of

a month's wages, unless the council permit smoking once a day before the mast and in no other place. (This rule may seem incomprehensible to modern people, but one must remember the constant fear of fire on board the old wooden ships, which were filled with all sorts of combustibles, not to mention the powder.)

48) Nobody shall be allowed to relieve himself except in the head or on the anchor next it. (The head was a projection under the bowsprit, where the large bower anchor was fastened securely outside the ship.) It must have been a cold and windy spot, in a fresh breeze constantly showered with flying spray and in heavy weather by the waves. Not a pleasant place to seek out and perhaps even dangerous on a dark stormy night. So there were men who tried to avoid it. Thus Jon Olafsson tells of the steward in the ship "Enhjørningen" who had neglected to go to the head in a storm and had instead relieved himself in the place where the bread was stored. Though the usual punishment for such an offence was keelhauling the steward was hanged from the bowsprit as an example because he had used the bread-room. It was always a recurrent problem, and as late as in Frederik V's articles for war at sea from 1752 we read: "Nobody shall pass water anywhere on board, nor besmirch the guns, gun-carriages, ship's gear or the like." Various punishments are mentioned: loss of wages, the cat-o'-nine tails, keelhauling, or, as in the steward's case, death.

60) If any man should rebel against the commander, the captain, or the merchant, no matter whether it be the master or the mate, or any other non-commissioned officer on shore or at sea, or if the common sailors or soldiers should rebel against the officers, whosoever they may be, they shall be punished by death without mercy according to the verdict of the ship's council.

87) Should any ships be taken by the Company's ships and men, then when all damages and expenses have been subtracted, and likewise the eighth part belonging to the crew, the rest shall be divided into two parts, one half to belong to Us and the other half to the Company.

(Given at Our Castle in Copenhagen October 16, 1639. Christian Rex.)

When the lengthy reading of the articles was concluded the trumpets sounded. The oath of allegiance was now read out to the assembled crews of the two ships after which they all raised three fingers and swore allegiance to King Christian and the East India Company.

After this the King had spoken both for himself and the Company; he thanked the brave seamen who were now setting out on this dangerous voyage for the common good, exhorted them to lead a godfearing life, to honest loyalty, a moral conduct, and brave deeds, to the glory of Denmark, and to their own honour and good name, so that other nations, both Christian and heathen, should find no occasion to speak ill of the Danes. The King then bared his head and prayed Heaven's blessing on the voyagers, that God would go with them in all their dealings both on land and at sea, both at home and abroad, to which prayer the whole assembly answered Amen. This ended the ceremony.

It is likely that the farewell to the *Christianshavn* and *The Gilded Sun* took place in much the same way that day in late October 1639. The officers and crew then put off in the boats to go on board their vessels. People waved and called out last greetings while the oarsmen tended to their oars. Now they passed Christian IV's almost completed Exchange, an imposing building with its shining copper roof and spire of intertwined dragons' tails, a landmark ready to greet the ships whenever they returned home. Only the eastern gable-wall was not yet finished. Just opposite stood the old anchor smithy which the King had converted into a church for the Royal Navy (Holmens Kirke) and behind that lay Bremerholm, the Naval Yard, with all its many activities necessary to keep the ships afloat and ready for service. And across the water to the south lay the new suburb the King had been building for the last twenty years, and which might almost be said to be the endeavour closest to his heart. Only last September he had made Christianshavn an independent borough, separate from Copenhagen with its own church, vicar, and corporation.

Above Copenhagen the Church of Our Lady reared its huge nave and the tower with its tall slender spire; in front of it was the fine Church of the Holy Spirit, and further east lay the Church of St Nicholas, a bit forlorn after its handsome octagonal spire had collapsed in the hurricane in 1628.

Soon the ships weighed their anchors and sailed north towards Elsinore. The Company had hired a pilot who was to conduct the ships safely through the Kattegat with its dangerous reefs and then across the North Sea to England. But as late as early November the ships were still lying behind Lappegrunden opposite Elsinore. The wind came from the northwest so there was no choice but to stay here till it changed. They made good use of the time to buy a number of items to complete their stores, and there was plenty of opportunity to supplement their victuals before the long voyage.

Copenhagen's harbour. To the left Christian IV's new harbour with the arsenal and victualling yard that equipped his warships. Today this is the garden of The Royal Library, where there still is a mooring ring in the wall to the right of the exit. In the middle of the picture can be seen Copenhagen Castle and the towers of the Church of Our Lady, St Petri, Helliggejst and Nikolaj. To the right the naval yard Holmen with the anchor smithy (now Holmen's Church), the long ropewalk and the sail loft. More ships are in the process of being built on the beach. (Engraving from a painting by Johan van Wick, ca. 1611. The National Museum, Copenhagen.)

On board *The Gilded Sun* a steady flow of new items was entered in the ledger quoted in rigsdaler, ort and skilling (1 ort = 1/4 rigsdaler, 1 rigsdaler = 24 skilling).

Paid for 1 fat lamb	1	–	–
1 cask fine ship's biscuits	2	2	1
Ink powder for Claus schoolmaster	3	3	20
6 leadlines	6	1	–
2 casks of barley for the chickens	3	–	–
10 dozen wooden spoons	–	2	12
2 red wooden bowls	–	1	–
18 brooms	–	–	18
Purchased 60 white cabbages for sauerkraut, 3 sk. each (1 sh. would have been fair) and for men to carry them up from the shore	1	3	20
Purchased 4 firkins beef as a treat for the men, they weighed 23 Lislb. 10 lb (about 378 pounds)	9	3	9
Paid for 18 Alen (about 36 ft.) drill for table-cloths in the cabin, as we formerly had only 3 table-cloths	–	4	2
Paid for red cabbages	1	2	18
As I had very little aqua vitae on board which could not be sufficient for so many people on so long a voyage I bought a hogshead of French spirits, and for the cabin a chest with all kinds of distilled spirits, for which I paid	52	–	–
Paid for 100 loaves called anchor stocks, for those given us at the victualling yard were mostly crumbled, as they had not been baked half enough Nobody could eat them.	7	–	–

For ten days the ships lay impatiently waiting for the weather to improve. Elsinore looked much as usual, now that the castle of Kronborg had been rebuilt after the destructive fire in 1629, its copper roofs shining against the scudding clouds. At last the wind shifted to the southwest, and on November 9 the two ships left the Sound. But they anchored again on November 11 at Varberg on the Swedish coast. On board *The Gilded*

Sun the meticulous ledger states that they here had to buy a new pair of snuffers for the binnacle, "as the old ones had fallen overboard".

Their stay here lasted over a fortnight, again because of the weather, but at last they started out again and managed to get out into the North Sea.

A strict discipline was maintained on board. The officers were to prevent all swearing, foul language and irreverent speech; the men were to listen to the chaplain's admonishing, and if any man should make fun of what was sacred he should be punished by death. Everybody was commanded to come to prayers, both morning and evening, when they heard the ship's bell.

It was winter; the days were short and murky. The sun could rarely be glimpsed, so that it was difficult to calculate an exact position, and they had to trust the Norwegian pilot to bring them safely to Plymouth in southern England. The wind became stronger, and one day it blew up to full storm, even a hurricane, a storm the likes of which none of the men on board could remember. Huge waves loosened the head on the *Christianshavn*. It wobbled from side to side and seemed about to go to pieces at any moment, so that they had to send men out with ropes to tie the planks together. It must have been a difficult task when the ship kept plunging its bows deep into the seas. The great waves rolled in over the forepeak so that the poor men had great trouble winding ropes around the rickety timbers and knotting them securely. They were so thoroughly exhausted and so stiff with cold after that job that they had to be helped in; but the job was done and the timbers stayed put.

So far the two ships had kept company; but during the hurricane the *Christianshavn* lost sight of *The Gilded Sun* somewhere south of the Dogger Bank. It was rumoured on board that their companion vessel had gone down with all hands. But the two ships were to rendezvous at Plymouth if they became separated, so one could only hope for the best.

All the hatches had of course been battened down during the storm; this meant that the air was heavy and the stench on the lower decks horrible. Several of the men suffered from seasickness; but worse still the scurvy had appeared. Among the sufferers, the corporal who commanded the troops was now seriously ill. On board the *Christianshavn* the cook Hans Sørensen had died before the ship left the Sound; but he had been ill already before they left Elsinore.

Even the worst storm finally blows itself out. This was followed by a flat calm. However, a thick fog now settled down, so dense that even the pilot had to admit that he could not tell their position until he could find a landmark of some kind. He threw out a lead with a lump of tallow on the bottom; when it was hauled in he studied the sand and small pebbles adhering to it and said he believed they were just off the Downs, the name given to the reefs off the coast of southeastern England. He actually declared that the fog was a blessing, for every captain was happy when his ship had passed safely through the Channel where the pirates from Dunkirk lay in wait and had through the years taken a number of good ships to the detriment of Danish shipping. But the pirates would have to be very lucky to find them in the thick fog.

At this time the Dunkirk pirates had become such a menace to shipping that Christian IV had recently sent his illegitimate son by Kirsten Madsdatter, young Christian Ulrik Gyldenløve, to the Cardinal Infante in Brussels in the Spanish Netherlands to demand restitution for the unlawful seizure of Danish ships. The Danish losses were estimated at more than 600,000 rigsdaler, a considerable sum. A few years earlier the king of Spain had proposed a treaty of commerce to the Danish king, and Christian was not unreceptive, but he had sworn that there could be no treaty until the Spaniards paid a substantial sum as an indemnity.

The Cardinal maintained that he had already written several times to the Spanish court about the matter, but had unfortunately received no answer. However, he thought that if the Danish king sent an ambassador to Madrid he would probably obtain what he demanded and they could then renew negotiations about the commercial treaty.

The *Christianshavn* was fortunate not to see anything of the pirates, and on January 10, 1640, the ship anchored in Plymouth road under the rolling green hill where Sir Francis Drake was said to have played bowls in 1588 while waiting to leave harbour for the battle with the Spanish Armada.

Only three days later *The Gilded Sun* appeared – the hurricane had blown it right up to the Norwegian coast, but it had suffered little damage. They now spent four weeks repairing the ships and obtaining new stores of victuals, water, and firewood for the galley. In spite of the severe punishment for deserting ship the bosun's mate, Thord Thorstensen, absconded from the *Christianshavn* and was lucky enough not to be caught.

In the *The Gilded Sun*'s ledger the list of purchases reckoned in rigsdaler, ort, and skilling grew:

1 bosun's silver pipe	9	2	–
Paid a town crier to proclaim in the town that nobody should give any member of our crew anything on credit	–	2	–
Gave our Norwegian pilot named Anders Pedersen expenses for his journey home	20	–	–
Bought for use in the cabin on the voyage 23 pounds fresh butter	2	1	20
For laundering the table cloths and napkins from the cabin	–	3	2
Paid a gentleman for 106 tuns of fresh water from the pump in his yard: 2 pence per tun	4	–	–
20 tuns of English beer	41	2	5
2 tuns of strong beer for the cabin	6	1	2
Spent on meals in Plymouth in our lodgings by me, the merchants, and the master when we sometimes went ashore, and the young governor and the captain of the castle were our guests twice	44	3	8
Paid during our entire stay for boats to transport goods to the ship, as I did not wish to risk our boat much ashore for fear our men would run	1	1	18

The above would seem to show that Claus Rytter himself kept the accounts – the "I" mentioned can hardly be other than himself.

Finally all the preparations were finished and on February 8 the voyage to the south continued. It is possible to form – though it must naturally be somewhat incomplete – a picture of life on board the *Christianshavn*. Before going on board the men had received two months' wages. As mentioned above the crew list has been preserved, and from this we can see that as commander Willem Leyel received 160 Dutch guilders a month, the master Jørgen Hansen 70, the chief mate Carsten Ludvigsen 80, the mate Peter de Siwart 50, the two merchants Philip de Goltz and Peter Lützen 40 and 35 respectively, the assistants between 12 and 15, the chief bosun Amund Olufsen 28, the steward Joost Petersen Panck 27, the barber Joakim Caulitz 20, the quartermasters 14. The common sailors got from 7 to 9 guilders each, and the ship's boys only 4-5.

To judge by the names, a number of these people were Dutch, and several had probably already made a number of voyages. The latter is certainly true of Leyel who had already made the voyage to the East a couple of times.

The crew was divided into two or three watches, and lists of the men's names were posted outside the captain's cabin. The day would usually be divided into six watches of four hours each. The watch was to take care of any work on board, mind the steering, row the boats, keep a lookout, keep the lanterns in working order, turn the sails in the locker to see they did not get mildewed, shake the gun powder so it did not become lumpy, sweep and wash down the decks every morning before the quarter that had the morning watch was roused. Often they had to take a turn at the pumps – almost all ships took in water.

There was a quartermaster in charge of each quarter; when his watch took over he had to call over the names of his men, share out the work and see that everything was done in an orderly fashion. The quartermaster had charge of the boats and had to keep everything shipshape. It was his responsibility that the cargo was safely stowed, and it was he who passed out the rations to the cook.

All on board shared the watches except the officers, the chaplain, and the merchants. Important decisions, such as the passing of sentences, etc., belonged to the ship's council, which seems to have been variously constituted, but as a rule it comprised the commander, the captain, the master, the mate, and the chief boatswain. There was also a larger council comprising officers from all the ships sailing together.

At this period the rudder was not yet in use; ships were still steered by means of the old-fashioned tiller. It was furnished with an auxiliary rope for use when it took several men to hold the tiller in a storm. In front of the helmsman the compass stood in its binnacle where a light burned all night. A special lamp trimmer was appointed to trim the lamp in the binnacle, the lanterns that shed their sleepy light below decks, and the great lantern in the stern of the ship that made it possible for the ships to keep together at night. The helmsman also had a half-hour glass in front of him so he could strike the half-hour on the ship's bell and then turn the glass. The next time he would strike two blows and so on, up to eight bells, which meant it was time for the other watch to take over.

The most important change was at 8 p.m. It began when the marshal struck a blow with his stick on the mainmast before which the watches were mustered. The watch coming on duty would be admonished to be alert, keep themselves from drink and do their duty. It was the custom that the youngest ship's boy then pronounced the old Catholic blessing

"Benedicite", after which they all sang a hymn and joined in a prayer asking God's protection from the dangers of the night, which were often real enough. The look-out and the helmsman were relieved, and the departing watch could go below and turn in.

On board the *Christianshavn* and the *Sun* all went well until the turn of the month when the ships were in the latitude of Madeira where Leyel, who now had a number of sick on board, had thought to seek harbour to refresh his men. But a new violent storm blew up, the two ships were parted, and the *Christianshavn*, which was now an old ship and had already been damaged by the storm in the North Sea, sprang several leaks and shipped more and more water. The men worked hard at the pumps, but it soon became clear that they must seek harbour.

The ship's council was hastily summoned, and their decision was entered in the journal:

"In the name of the Lord we the undersigned ship's council in the ship Christianshavn" gathered to resolve as follows: Whereas the "Sun" the past night near the island of Teneriffa has been lost from view, and we with the present ship the "Christianshavn" were near the above mentioned island on a lea shore in a violent storm and were forced to sail east of the said island we decided to go in to Santa Cruz, which is the nearest harbour and hope there to await the "Sun" if it can hold the same course. There we shall endeavour to plug the five big leaks we have in the ship, two in the bows, and three behind the mainmast, and at the same time to procure at the said town Santa Cruz lemons, bitter oranges, and other necessaries for the refreshment of our sick and other things; that we are thus resolved we affirm with our own hands. Signed in the ship 'Christianshavn' in the morning about 7 o'clock March 3, 1640".

Thus the *Christianshavn* was alone when it anchored at about 5 a.m. in the road north of the town. A little later a polite Spanish officer was rowed out to them to inquire who they were, where the ship came from and where they were going. When Leyel had given the required information the officer said that they were welcome to stay and would of course be given any assistance they required, only they should send a man ashore with the ship's papers.

As the chief merchant Philip de Goltz spoke excellent Spanish he was sent ashore to show the King's pass and to ask for assistance to repair the ship, and to ask for fruit and vegetables for the sick. Leyel was rather anxious about the outcome as he knew that the Spaniards were opposed to letting other nations enter the lands in the East which, they maintained, the Pope by his bull in 1493 had bestowed upon the Portuguese, and now that Portugal belonged under the Spanish crown Spain intended to use all the power at its command to defend this right. On the other hand, even the Spaniards must know that both the Dutch and the English, and now also the Danes, had colonies in the East, and that their East India Companies were regularly sending ships out to them.

So he was not greatly surprised when another Spanish officer shortly appeared demanding that the captain should come ashore to give a fuller explanation of where the ship belonged and what their destination was. So Captain Jørgen Hansen Riber was sent ashore together with the steward Joost Petersen Panck as interpreter.

In the meantime the men on board worked feverishly to repair the damages caused by the storm; it might become necessary to sail at short notice. Leyel's unrest must have increased as the hours passed – there were rumours that the three men had been taken inland to the Spanish governor's residence somewhere in the interior of the island.

By the afternoon of March 5 his unrest was replaced by certainty when Pedersen Panck returned with a command from the commander of the fort at Santa Cruz that Commander Leyel himself and the chief mate should both report to him.

Leyel sought to gain time by saying that it was late, he would have to remain on board that night; he would then come the next morning, but it would be unfortunate if all the ship's officers were gone at the same time. So he would gladly come, but not before the others were on board again.

But Leyel had already decided what he was going to do. They must try to get away as soon as it was dark that evening, otherwise they might be delayed indefinitely. He hated to leave any of his people, especially the captain whom he valued highly; but it was either that or risk giving up the entire voyage. The only comfort was that Claus Rytter seemed to have sailed on and could bring relief to Tranquebar.

That evening Leyel got his launch ready as though he were making ready to obey the commander's orders the following morning. But in the middle of the night when the town was completely dark and even the soldiers in the fort seemed to be asleep, the two boats were manned and equipped with towropes. There was almost no wind, and the faint breeze there was blew in from the sea. The boats were needed to help the ship get under sail. It would make too much noise to heave the anchor so they cut the hawser and began to take the ship in tow.

For some time it seemed that they would be able to make their escape; the boats' crews were taken on board and the boats towed behind the ship. The sails had already begun to draw and the ship moved noiselessly towards the open sea. But suddenly they saw soldiers with burning torches on the ramparts, shouted commands could be heard, shortly followed by cannon shots. The first shot hissed past the *Christianshavn*; but the second struck the ship on the port side in the aftermost part of the gun-room and shattered the tiller so the ship could no longer be steered. The Spanish gunners had apparently found the range and now every shot found its mark.

An iron cannon ball of 24 pounds struck off a piece of the mizzenmast, a second made a hole two feet above the water line, a third removed a large piece of the foreyard. An even larger ball weighing 36 pounds made a hole only one foot above the waterline. They were also shot at from the opposite side by a Spanish ship, but with little damage.

Leyel had forbidden his men to shoot. If they got off all would be well; but if they did not succeed the situation would become impossible if they were found guilty of firing at a royal Spanish fortress. He had no authority to take such drastic measures. When it became clear that there was no hope of getting clear of the harbour in their partially wrecked ship he gave orders to hoist a white flag as a sign of surrender.

On seeing this the Spaniards stopped shooting and sent a captain on board with orders to Commander Leyel, the mate, and all the officers to come ashore immediately – if they did not at once comply with these orders the ship would be sunk. So there was nothing for it. Leyel went down to his cabin to fetch the King's "Salvum conductum" so he could hand it to the Spanish commander together with a protest against the violence done to his ship.

Together with his chief mate Carsten Ludvigsen and twenty-two other men Leyel was now escorted up to the commander of the fortress where Leyel sought to hand over the King's pass to show that he sailed on a legitimate errand for his King and had done nothing that could justify the Spaniards in detaining the ship, let alone shooting at it.

However, the commander refused to listen to him, but referred to his orders from the governor commanding him to send Leyel, together with the captain, the mate, and chief merchant, to the governor's residence in the island's capital La Laguna about five miles inland from Santa Cruz.

So next morning they set off guarded by a detachment of Spanish soldiers. That evening Leyel was closely examined by the governor who refused to accept Leyel's explanations. He was sceptical of the idea that the Danish king had a colony and a fortress on the coast of India. This could simply not be true as everybody knew that by the Pope's decision India belonged to the Portuguese, and now that Portugal in 1580 had become a part of the Spanish kingdom it belonged to Spain. No other nation had any right to settle there. Hence all Leyel's explanations were simply a pack of lies. The governor felt that there was something decidedly fishy about the whole business. Were these men pirates or foreign merchants trying to force their way into Spanish domains? He commanded that the Danes be held as prisoners under heavy guard that night.

The next day Leyel managed to get hold of a lawyer to take his case, and a notary who made a copy of the King's pass which he delivered to the governor. He dared not risk the original out of his possession.

But nothing seemed to make any impression on the governor. He merely shrugged his shoulders. His Majesty, the Spanish king, certainly intended to prevent any ships but his own from sailing to all the countries in the East. At any rate, he maintained that the Danish king's pass was not worth the paper it was written on.

Leyel protested that this was by no means the first Danish expedition to go to India. For the past twenty years King Christian had owned the fortress Dansborg on the Coast of Coromandel, and the Danish East India Company had a number of trading stations scattered around the East and had for the last twenty years sent ships that had completed their voyage out and home with no opposition. Besides His Excellency could not be ignorant of the fact that both the English and the Dutch had a number of fortresses and trading stations throughout the East, so the governor must be completely out of touch with reality if he thought he could prevent everyone except the Spaniards from trading there.

But the haughty governor, Don Luis Fernandez de Cordoba, refused to listen to any argument. He simply reiterated that if Leyel was so sure he was right and convinced that he was doing no wrong, then why had he tried to sneak out of the harbour in the night? This hardly indicated a clear conscience. An honest man sails out by daylight; only thieves and robbers sneak out of a harbour in the middle of the night. Leyel replied that he had feared, as was now the case, that he would be prevented from leaving, and he felt that he owed his King, whose servant he was, to do his utmost to complete the voyage the King had entrusted to him.

But it was to no avail. The governor merely looked haughtily at the angry Dane and maintained that he was merely acting according to his instructions. If Mr Leyel wished to complain he was at liberty to go to Madrid and lodge a complaint with the king, and if he did not himself wish to make the journey, he could send one of his men with a power of attorney. But he should not expect that the outcome would be any different in Madrid.

Leyel, who knew something of Spanish bureaucracy was in despair. To try and get the case heard in Madrid would take months, perhaps even years, and in the meantime the *Christianshavn* was to lie and rot at Santa Cruz, while the crew deteriorated because of idleness, illness, and desertion. He might just as well give up the whole voyage. In the depths of his depression he scarcely heard the governor's merciless voice saying that the Spaniards would of course have to impound the ship's sails and rudder to prevent further attempts at flight. He also intended to put all the trading goods and arms in storage, and finally he must request Señor Leyel to hand over all ready money together with the Danish passes and letters, for which his officials would give him a receipt. But if Leyel wished to go to Madrid to complain he would grant him 600 rigsdaler of his own money for the trip. In the meantime the crew would be treated as prisoners on board the ship, and Spanish soldiers would be posted to keep guard of the *Christianshavn* or *Christianopuerto* as the Spaniards called it.

A crestfallen Leyel returned to his ship still under guard and with an official who came on board with him and demanded that he hand over the money and papers. A number of soldiers were detailed to supervise the unloading of the items mentioned by the governor. The guns were left where they stood, but were of course of no use without powder and cannon balls.

Leyel now took counsel with his officers, and they decided that he should go to Madrid together with Philip de Goltz, who could speak Spanish, and one of the assistants Niels Rasmussen, while the captain Jørgen Hansen Riber was to stay behind and was given the responsibility for the ship and crew left behind at Tenerife.

On March 16 the three Danes left Santa Cruz under the guard of a Spanish capitan de guarda Don Pedro Flores in a small caravel. The voyage was not without its dangers, for the ship got into difficulties off the Barbary coast, where they feared to be taken prisoner and made slaves. After that the ship was delayed by contrary winds, so that they did not get ashore near Gibraltar until late April. Their fears off the coast of Barbary were not groundless. Many ships through the years had been captured by pirates from Algeria and Morocco, who then sold those on board as slaves. One of these unfortunates was probably the Icelander Jonas, who in 1646 had to make a public confession in the Navy Church in Copenhagen because, having lived for 18-20 years in Barbary, he had let himself be circumcised, which presumably means that he had converted to Islam.

In Madrid Leyel at once lodged a complaint about the treatment he had received and demanded on behalf of the Danish king that the *Christianshavn* be released at once so that he could continue his voyage. The Spanish officials would not commit themselves, begged him to have patience and shelved the matter. Leyel also sought out the Danish agent in the city, and together they repeatedly visited the authorities or asked for an audience with the king. They were always received with the utmost politeness, but the men in charge shrugged their shoulders and said the matter must follow the usual channels; they could do nothing, it had already been sent on to the next office, etc. Before any action could be taken it had to be submitted to the king's powerful Prime Minister Don Gasparo de Guzman with the impressive titles Count of Olivarez and Duke of San Lucar de Barrameda; he would then forward it to the Council of State, from where it would be passed on to the Navy Office, and from there to the Ministry for War.

The weeks passed and the weeks became months. Leyel had almost reached the last of his 600 rigsdaler, and after they were gone what could he and his two companions live on? It was unfortunate that the Danish agent was not much esteemed in Madrid; but Leyel had also begun to realize that the governor of Tenerife, Don Luis Fernandez, who was a knight of the exclusive Order of St James, belonged to a very influential family with relatives in important offices all over the administration, men who were proud to maintain that the governor had done his king a valuable service by arresting the Danish ship.

In the meantime Leyel learned much about the Spanish love of paperwork. The official documents in several copies snailed their way from the Consejo de Guerra to the Consejo de Almirantazgo and on to the Consejo de Justicia and the Consejo de Estada, and were then passed on to Count Olivares and back again. Time after time work was held up because of the many Catholic festivals and religious processions. Leyel was out of patience. Each day was not only wasted – yet another lump of lead weighing down on his restless energy – but he knew that day by day the expenses for victualling the crew on the *Christianshavn* increased by another 100 ducats. If this was to go on – and there seemed to be no end in sight – he would end up with a partially wrecked ship and no capital whatever and would have to give up any thought of completing his voyage to India; indeed, in the end he would probably lose the ship. This was not to be borne.

On the other hand he could see that the Spanish government had its hands full. There was rebellion in Catalonia, where the citizens of Barcelona had taken the Spanish general prisoner, dragged him through the streets and then killed him and burned the king's bailiff to death in his house with all his servants. And a Spanish fleet on its way to the West Indies had been attacked by a French fleet off Cadiz; the Spanish admiral's ship had caught fire and half a dozen of the other vessels had been captured and the rest badly damaged.

In July it was rumoured that the Consejo de Justicia had discovered that Leyel's pass and his "Salvum conductum" were forgeries, that the whole crew were Dutch, or, there were at least a great number of Dutchmen on board – and the Spaniards were at war with the Netherlands. They also maintained that the Danish king could not possibly have a fortress in India. Hence everything Leyel had said was a pack of lies and hence the Spaniards intended to confiscate both his ship and its cargo.

Apart from this impending catastrophe Leyel's immediate situation was desperate. He had no more money. He appealed to some merchants that he knew had dealings with the wealthy merchant Johan Braëm in Copenhagen. The latter was one of the directors of the Company, so it would have been natural for him to help Leyel in his difficulties. One of these merchants did agree to make him a loan of 350 Spanish reals, but unfortunately the man died a few days later before the loan had been made, and Leyel no longer knew where to turn. He wrote home that one could not appeal to the officials without offering them substantial bribes, and he now barely had enough for daily bread for himself and his two companions.

But just when things looked completely hopeless it was reported that Hannibal Sehested, who had been chosen to be one of Christian IV's sons-in-law, had arrived at the port of Coruña at the head of a Danish delegation.

Leyel had of course written home about his difficulties, and Sehested had also been given orders to assist him; but there was another reason for the arrival of the Danish envoy. In 1638 and 1639 Christian IV had increased the Sound Dues, something which had of course infuriated the Dutch. As a counterbalance to the Netherlands he had then thought of the possibility of entering into an alliance with Spain. Furthermore, as already mentioned, when Christian IV's son Ulrik Christian Gyldenløve had negotiated with the Cardinal Infante in the Spanish Netherlands and complained of the many Danish ships captured by the Dunkirk pirates Christian IV had been recommended to apply directly to King Philip IV. It had then been said that Spain was ready to enter into an alliance with Denmark. The problems with the Dunkirk pirates had become more and more urgent. Their incursions into Danish waters were numerous: in 1628 they had taken a Danish galley in the southern part of the Lillebælt near Assens; in 1635 a Spanish pirate had impudently cruised near Skagen looking for prizes; and once when the King was cruising off Flekkerø near Christianssand in Norway he found that two of his captains simply refused to attack a Dunkirk ship, for which he had them both laid in irons that night.

So King Christian had now taken the Cardinal's advice and sent a richly furnished delegation. He wanted to show the conceited Spaniards that His Danish Majesty was a force to be reckoned with. Counting the pages and servants, the delegation numbered seventy men, many of whom belonged to the nobility. There was another of the King's illegitimate sons, Hans Ulrik Gyldenløve, and several noblemen, such as the two brothers Mogens and Eiler Ulfeldt, Erik Rosenkrantz, and Otto Krag. Two navy vessels had transported the delegation to Spain.

On Sehested's arrival a little comedy as to the right of precedence was enacted. The Prime Minister, the Count Olivares, had introduced the custom that all ambassadors were to call him "Your Excellency", whereas he never used that form of address to them. Other ambassadors had put up with this arrogant treatment, but Hannibal Sehested refused to accept it. Four years earlier Sehested had become engaged to Christian IV's daughter Christiane, who was only ten years old at the time, and as the King's personal representative and future son-in-law he considered himself of just as high rank as the Spanish king. Olivares asked him rather crossly why he could not accept this treatment, to which even the Emperor's delegate had agreed. But, wrapped in all sorts of courteous compliments, Sehested insisted that as the representative of the Danish king he could not agree to this.

Olivares finally gave in to Sehested's demands, and the latter now made a splendid entry into Madrid. Four richly caparisoned horses led the procession, a gift from Christian IV to the Spanish king. The Spaniards now showered honours on Sehested. He was lodged in a palace belonging to the king, and the king paid for his and his escorts' food and drink. Both Olivares and other Spanish grandees paid him the first visit – a rare compliment. A special bullfight was arranged, and it was announced that it took place in honour of the Danish ambassador.

The Emperor's ambassador had just died; but the Pope's nuntius and the Polish and Venetian ambassadors all protested against the preferential treatment given to the Dane at their expense and in disparagement of their masters, but the Spaniards answered that this was a matter for the host nation to decide and referred to an ancient "lex hospitii".

Behind the flattering treatment was of course the Spanish wish to conclude an offensive and defensive alliance with Denmark. At this time King Philip was at war both with France and the province of Holland. As already mentioned Catalonia was in open rebellion, and the Portuguese were more and more threatening in their demands to have their own king. So Philip would welcome Danish assistance, especially from the powerful Danish navy, and he was willing to go to great lengths to obtain it.

On November 3 Sehested was granted an audience with Philip IV, where he conveyed the greetings of his king to Philip, the Queen, the young Infante, and Count Olivares. An amusing detail was that Sehested insisted on keeping his hat on his head during the audience. So when King Philip greeted him they both removed their hats at the same time, but immediately put them on again. Sehested could not speak Spanish, but was fairly fluent in Italian, as he had formerly accompanied one of Christian IV's sons Valdemar Christian on his grand tour, which went both to France and Italy. Hence the two gentlemen could converse without an interpreter. But the conversation was more or less confined to the usual compliments, and Sehested was requested to hand in the confidential messages he had from his king in writing.

Leyel naturally went to seek out Sehested without delay. The latter could report that Leyel's letters had been received in Copenhagen and that King Christian had been very angry at the treatment of the *Christianshavn* on Tenerife. The King had specially charged him to see to it that the ship was released so that the interrupted voyage to India could be resumed.

As Leyel was still short of money he ventured to ask whether Sehested could not advance him some money on behalf of the East India Company. Sehested, however, refused, as he did not feel himself empowered to dispose of the Company's funds. He suggested instead that Leyel take up a private loan from him of 500 reals and sign an undertaking that he or his heirs be held responsible for that sum if the Company should refuse to reimburse Sehested. Leyel had to agree to these conditions, though he stipulated that his wife must not thus be left destitute.

Sehested then related some of the difficulties the delegation had faced on the voyage due to an impossible pilot. The ship had now and then been in grave difficulties due to the pilot's stupidity and inexperience; but they had several times had better luck than they deserved. Towards the end they had sailed a whole day along the coast of Galicia without the least idea of where they were or where they could find a harbour. Sehested had finally been forced to send Eiler Ulfeldt ashore with a boat to inquire as to their whereabouts. He returned with a Spanish pilot who brought them in to Vivero, whose inhabitants fled in terror at the sight of the ship. They had thought it belonged to raiding Turkish pirates. A few days later they had finally reached Coruña.

In Madrid Sehested now handed over the Danish written complaint over Spanish offences. It was divided into four sections:

1) Danish subjects had repeatedly during the last seventeen years suffered grave injustices in Spain. 2) During the same period the so-called Dunkirk captains had with barefaced effrontery taken Danish ships, even in Danish waters. 3) Many Danish and Norwegian ships had been seized by the Spaniards at a great loss to the owners and to the cost of the seamen. 4) Finally, there was the outrageous treatment accorded to the Danish ship *Christianshavn* at Tenerife, a matter which Commander Leyel for the last six months had tried to have rectified in Madrid.

The Spanish secretary of state who later discussed these complaints with Sehested was plainly disappointed. Four grievances, but no positive suggestions. The Spaniards had counted on proposals for a Danish–Spanish commercial treaty, or perhaps even a defensive alliance, and here the Danish ambassador merely voiced his grievances over a number of, to say the least, rather unimportant issues. Sehested insisted that the Danish king considered it a very serious matter that the his ships for no reason at all, and completely illegally, were being seized and his subjects imprisoned, even killed and robbed of their goods.

He hinted that they might at a later date enter into negotiations with regard to the subjects the secretary had mentioned, but not before the four grievances he had mentioned had been redressed. The Danish and Norwegian ships that had been seized in Spanish harbours must be released; there were large claims for damages; and the governor of Tenerife, who had illegally seized the King's ship and prevented Commander Leyel and his men from continuing their lawful voyage, must be removed and summoned to Madrid to answer for his actions. It was time to make an example: the Spanish governor had fired on the Danish king's ship, done his utmost to have the ship confiscated and sent Commander Leyel under guard to Madrid where he now for six months had sought the assistance of the Spanish authorities without any result.

The secretary felt that the Spaniards were within their rights in detaining the *Christianshavn* as the ship's pass had evidently been forged, there were several Dutchmen on board both as officers and common seamen; and it had been proved that Leyel had corresponded with the Dutch. Furthermore, the ship had attempted to sneak out of the harbour at night, and finally, it was common knowledge that only Spaniards had the right to sail to India.

Sehested calmly rejected most of these claims and also pointed out that the governor of Tenerife was hardly to be trusted. At least Leyel had received the impression that the matter could have been adjusted if he had paid him a sufficiently large bribe, a condition he had been unable to accept.

In the weeks following Sehested had to use all his talents to cope with the Spanish delaying tactics. He threatened that if the Spaniards would not make restitution for the enormous losses the Danes had suffered through Spanish wrongdoing, the King would have to forbid all Danish merchantmen to call at Spanish ports and at the same time see to it that all the ships from the Netherlands and the Hanseatic towns that passed through the Sound did not carry goods to Spain. Finally, he could give his ships letters of marque with the right to seize Spanish ships. Denmark's trade with Spain had mostly to do with the import of salt, and this he could obtain elsewhere.

For a long time nothing much seemed to happen, and Leyel sometimes despaired. One day he went up to Sehested with a letter he had received from the officers on the *Christianshavn*, in which they told of how the general of the fortress at Santa Cruz, soon after Leyel had left Tenerife, had removed all the dried fish they had on board as well as a large part of the equipment such as cordage and sailcloth, and had had it sold on the island by means of an ill-mannered Spaniard called Domingo Lambrana. When the Danes ventured to protest, he merely answered that the ship no longer belonged to the King of Denmark, but to His Spanish Majesty, and he had even threatened Jørgen Hansen with a stick if he resisted.

He had also beaten several Danish sailors, merely because they stood looking on while the Spaniards removed equipment and victuals from the ship. The same gentleman had also forbidden the local inhabitants to lend the Danes horses or mules so that they could ride in to Laguna to lodge a complaint against his actions. Nevertheless, a few of the sailors had slipped away at night on foot in order to request the governor to protect them from the fellow's insulting manners and his plundering of their ship – but with no result.

Sehested admitted that these were grave insults, but asked Leyel to be patient a while longer. The Spaniards would be forced to make good all the Danish losses. For he was in no doubt that Philip was very keen to obtain a treaty of Danish military assistance and would go to great lengths to obtain it. It was common knowledge that the Spanish king had his own difficulties. In 1639 the annual silver fleet from America did not cross the Atlantic, and he was in great need of the money. The court maintained an extravagant and showy lifestyle that would have horrified Philip's grandfather, the grave and deeply religious Philip II. One financial crisis came hard on the heels of the previous one, and the political unrest in both Catalonia and Portugal constantly threatened to destroy his power.

But now and again Sehested had to admit that he, too, lost patience with the slow Spanish administration. They kept demanding fresh documents. He was requested to put a figure to the total damages the Spaniards and the Dunkirk pirates had caused Danish and Norwegian shipping. Fortunately he had in his possession a list beginning with the seizure in 1622 of four Danish ships belonging to Jan Ettersen and company, all citizens of Copenhagen. The ships had been on the way to Ribadeos in Galicia. The first of these vessels was named *Den romerske Kirke* (*The Roman Church*), and the damages with interest amounted to 14,500 rigsdaler. And the list continued year by year ending with the *Raphael* belonging to Søren Christensen, a citizen of Marstrand. It had in 1639 been seized in Lisbon and sent to Brazil with Spanish and Portuguese officers to command her. Here damages were set at 12,000 rigsdaler.

But even after the papers had been handed in it always took a long time before anything happened. The matter was sent from one office to the next, to the Council of Ministers, to Count Olivares, to the King, and then back again. Weeks passed.

But at last, in early December, Sehested's perseverance bore fruit. The King now said that the *Christianshavn* could be released, and promised that the governor of Tenerife would be summoned to Madrid to be examined as to his conduct. But Sehested was still not satisfied. He produced an estimate of the damages suffered by the Danish king and the East India Company because of the ship's being detained at Tenerife for ten months reckoned from March 15, 1640:

Wages for the men on the *Christianshavn* (74 persons)	10,000 rdl.
Victuals for the men at Tenerife (74 persons)	10,650 rdl.
Victuals for Willem Leyel and two men in Madrid	2500 rdl.
Damages and delay of voyage	25,000 rdl.
Maintenance of the ship	5000 rdl.
In all: 53,150 rigsdaler.	

In addition to this there was the cost of the things the Spaniards had removed from the *Christianshavn*, a list Lützen had made out from the inventory the governor himself had had made when the ship was seized. The prices were in Spanish reals:

4 buoy ropes, each 5 inches thick and 30 fathoms long	1110
1750 pounds of pork	1750
1565 dried fish	1520
1 chest with tallow candles	225
4 muskets	128
25 lanterns	200
with many other things. In all 79,710 reals.	

With these papers Sehested again sought an audience with the king, where he pointed out that the governor's rude treatment of the Danish king's own ship was now known throughout Europe, and that hence King Christian must demand a speedy settlement that could give his commander full satisfaction for the insult. Sehested repeated that Leyel had done nothing wrong, but had nevertheless been sent to Madrid where he had for six months lived a wretched life and not been able to obtain justice. The *Christianshavn* must now speedily be released, the governor be punished, the impounded – if not to say stolen – goods be returned, and the damages made good to Willem Leyel either in ready money or in bills of exchange on Lisbon.

The Duke of Olivares maintained that Christian IV should not send ships to the East without first apprising the Spanish king; but just as Leyel had previously informed the governor, Sehested now had to inform the Spaniards that Denmark was not the least interested in the Pope's arbitrary division of the world. The oceans were free, and any ship could sail wherever it pleased. And the Danish king had now for the last twenty years owned a fortress in Tranquebar on the Coast of Coromandel and should therefore have the right to send his ships there.

When Sehested was asked to name a figure for all the Danish claims he replied that the damages caused by both the Spaniards and the Dunkirk pirates to Danish and Norwegian shipping amounted to 524,000 rigsdaler. But there were also claims for sixty-four illegally detained ships amounting to nearly the same figure. However, he was willing to drop the latter point and be content with 500,000 rigsdaler. But of course this would be besides the damages for the seizing of the *Christianshavn*.

After another round of negotiations the two parties seemed to be on the brink of coming to a reasonable agreement, though the Spaniards demanded that the whole question of Denmark's right to send ships to India be negotiated between the two monarchs. It was also necessary for Sehested to repeat his demands regarding the *Christianshavn*: Willem Leyel and his ship must be released, the ship in the same condition as when it had been seized, all Leyel's letters and documents must be returned, and he must be provided with the necessary papers so he could continue his voyage and be given facilities to have his ship repaired at a Spanish dockyard and provided with the necessary provisions. Finally, the governor of Tenerife must be removed and punished for his illegal activities.

When the Spaniards were slow to agree to these conditions Sehested stated that he was not going to alter any of his demands. If the Spaniards did not wish to agree to them they would have to give up all thought of a Danish-Spanish treaty, and he would then leave for Bilbao to embark for home. This convinced them.

On February 27 Leyel was given all the letters that had been taken from him, together with the necessary documents and passes for him to continue his voyage. But even here there were problems. The Minister for War and the President of the Portuguese Council wished to keep all Leyel's letters, instructions, and ship's articles so as to have them translated and see if they permitted Leyel to trade on the west coast of India where the Portuguese had traded for more than a century. It was only when Sehested complained directly to the king that the latter gave his personal orders that all the documents should immediately be handed over to Leyel. Sehested also saw to it that Leyel was given a new pass and money enough to have the ship repaired, manned and provisioned.

It was March 12 before the final treaty between the two countries was approved by King Philip, whose serious illness had further delayed the matter. The subjects of the Danish king were to have free access to trade and to visit Spanish ports on a par with Spain's other allies, the right to appoint Danish consuls in a number of ports, and the illegal attacks on Danish ships must cease. As to the amount of damages demanded by Sehested the Spaniards maintained that owing to the present unrest in the kingdom they were unable to pay any damages to Denmark in ready money as Sehested had bargained for. But in order to show their desire for friendship with Denmark Spain would deliver salt to a value of 100,000 rigsdaler duty free – the freedom from duty they estimated to be worth another 225,000 rigsdaler. Thus the total was still a good bit below the 500,000 rigsdaler demanded by Sehested. However, he declared himself satisfied, and the money was to be paid over a lengthy period in "white and granulated" salt. The Spaniards also promised that Don Luis Fernandez de Cordoba would be removed, though in order to save face it was made to appear that it was for other reasons than the treatment of the Danish ship.

After successfully having completed his mission, Hannibal Sehested left Madrid on May 9 and journeyed home via Paris and London. Hans Ulrik Gyldenløve had already been sent home as he had suffered an attack of epilepsy immediately after the bullfight, and it was thought it would be better to treat him at home. But Eiler Ulfeldt remained behind in Madrid as the Danish resident, with the task among other things of obtaining a concession from the Spaniards giving Danish merchants the right to free trade in the East.

CHAPTER 5
OBSTACLES

It was with a great sigh of relief that Leyel could finally bid farewell to Madrid, where he had wasted nearly a year. He had with him letters from the Spanish king to the Audiencia of all ministers and officials on the Canary Islands and to Don Luis Fernandez with strict orders to release the *Christianshavn* with all its equipment. He also had a money order on a Don Juan de la Calle in Seville for 4000 pieces-of-eight with which to buy provisions and other necessities for the voyage. Leyel therefore spent some weeks in that town while he bought beef, fish, peas, oil, rice, a little butter, and cloth for the men. He succeeded likewise in recruiting six seamen in Seville, but had to give up finding a new carpenter. The merchant Philip de Goltz, who probably was Dutch, seems to have been afraid of returning to the Canaries, where the authorities had begun to ask too many questions about his past, so he asked Leyel for permission to leave the service. Leyel could not agree to this; Goltz had sworn to serve during the whole voyage. De Goltz then applied to Sehested, who told Leyel that the new treaty with Spain did not allow any Dutchman to act in the Danish king's service in the so-called Spanish countries. As a result de Goltz was discharged in Madrid.

On May 20 a happy Leyel sailed in an English ship from Cadiz with his men and his goods, and after an easy voyage he could present a shaken Don Luis with the King's letter ordering him immediately to release the *Christianshavn* together with all its equipment and the ready money he had seized. However, it was not that simple. The governor managed to find any number of excuses and made so many difficulties that Leyel had to seek legal assistance.

The fact was that the governor was unable to hand over the money he had seized as it was no longer in his possession. He had gone into partnership with two clever Dutch merchants who in spite of the war between Spain and the Netherlands had managed to establish a flourishing business on Tenerife. In 1630 Christian IV had concluded a treaty with the Spanish commissary Gabriel de Roy allowing ships from Glückstadt that were in possession of a pass and a recommendation from de Roy to trade freely with Spanish lands. Under cover of this, and trading under the Danish flag and invoking Glückstadt's privileges, the two Dutchmen had made quite a fortune, and the governor had hoped to secure a substantial profit by entrusting most of Leyel's money to them.

Leyel now ran into fresh difficulties as he found out that all the lawyers on the island refused to help him for fear of the governor. However, he found a single man willing to counsel him. This was a Don Diego Llarena Maldonado, a man who for a number of years had lived in France, England, and the Netherlands, and who during Leyel's absence had been of some assistance to Jørgen Hansen. Not even Don Diego dared appear publicly, but wrote the legal document Leyel was to present to the Audiencia on Gran Canaria to force them to implement the king's order. Leyel had himself to make out a fair copy of the document, have it signed by a priest, who had taken a legal degree, but was not subject to the governor's jurisdiction. Leyel had to run from pillar to post and was furious at the difficulties caused by the governor.

In spite of the king's promises to Sehested the governor still seemed to be doing everything in his power to put obstacles in Leyel's way. Even a year after Sehested in Madrid had been given assurances that everything was now in order the Danish Chancellery notes on March 22, 1642, that they have been informed that the *Christianshavn* is still being detained at Tenerife by the governor in spite of the promises given by the Spanish king, so that they must request Eiler Ulfeldt, who had remained in Madrid, to complain to King Philip. One can see from the *Christianshavn*'s accounts that Leyel had to make at least two trips to Gran Canaria to demand that the authorities there take action against the pigheaded Don Luis, who was naturally furious at the difficulties this officious Danish commander continued to cause him.

At last, on November 18, Leyel declared himself content with the return of provisions, implements, weapons, and ammunition, and, as a partial compensation for the missing money, the governor handed over thirty-two chests of Brazilian sugar. Leyel thought at first that he could sell the sugar locally; but he only succeeded in disposing of six of the chests. Two other chests, that together weighed 1600 pounds, were ruined when they tried to hoist them on board. The rope broke, and one of the chests fell into the boat which was swamped so that all the sugar in both chests was ruined.

Sehested had asked Leyel to send his assistant Niels Rasmussen home to Copenhagen with the news as soon as his outstanding account with Don Luis was settled. So Niels Rasmussen was given a letter with all Leyel's news and travelled home by England with the remaining twenty-four chests of sugar, in all 19,320 pounds, which Leyel thought the Company could sell at a much better profit in Copenhagen.

Leyel wrote that only one man had died on board. But four others had drowned, the steward Joost Petersen had deserted, and there had been serious problems with Svend Nielsen, who in Leyel's absence had refused to obey Jørgen Hansen, threatened to strike him before the assembled crew, and tried to raise a mutiny. As punishment he had been keelhauled, his month's wages had been confiscated and he had been put ashore. The chaplain, Lauritz Caspersen, had also caused trouble. He had proved to be much too fond of the excellent Canary wine when ashore, got drunk and then became quarrelsome or violent and destroyed everything in his path. Leyel wrote that they had more difficulties with him than with any of the others; he had finally had to forbid him to go ashore. Finally, one man had deserted ship at Plymouth, and about thirty had found means to run during the long stay at Santa Cruz and later at Cadiz.

After the long delay at Tenerife the *Christianshavn* was in such poor condition that Leyel found it necessary to have it repaired in a shipyard. However, as there were no such facilities at Tenerife, he intended to sail the ship to Cadiz where he would also be able to find replacements for the ropes, cables, etc., sold by the governor. Finally, he also lacked a good longboat and some victuals, especially dried cod, as the governor had removed the ship's entire supply. As an efficient merchant Leyel offered a Spanish captain to carry his goods for him to Cadiz, and he likewise took several people on board as passengers so that he calculated on a profit of more than 5000 pieces-of-eight, which would mean that he could make the Spanish voyage without any expense to the Company.

All the ship's casks and barrels were in the meantime stored in a warehouse and left in the care of one of the assistants, Johan Poelman, and the ship's cooper. Shortly before New Year 1642 the *Christianshavn* entered Cadiz where work was immediately begun. Leyel wrote out detailed instructions for Jørgen Hansen and the ship's council for them to have the ship careened and repaired, buy stores for five months at sea and find a good ship's carpenter, who was ready to make the voyage with them. And finally Hansen was to buy a quantity of wine. Leyel left him 758 pieces-of-eight to cover the costs and then left for Madrid where he sought out Eiler Ulfeldt, or Don Hilario as the Spaniards called him.

As a mere curiosity it appears that Leyel had brought ten dozen canaries with him from the Islands as presents for Eiler Ulfeldt, Johan Braëm, and others; but, sad to say, all but two had perished on the voyage.

In Spain the winter weather was severe and the roads practically impassable, so that it was February 13 before Leyel arrived in the city. Here he described to Ulfeldt the governor's dishonest practices and his difficulty in obtaining the money owed him. The two of them succeeded in getting the Spanish government to write even stricter orders to Don Luis. With some difficulty Leyel managed to get permission to see the documents, and he writes joyfully that they contained many reprimands of the governor for his unjustifiable treatment of the Danish commander and his ship and demanded that he make full restitution of everything he had removed from the ship.

By May 4 Leyel was again in Cadiz, where the *Christianshavn* was ready, the goods they lacked had been purchased, and everything made ready for them to leave. However, it was not that simple. The drunken chaplain had been involved in fighting and public attacks on the officers, so that Leyel thought it best to put him ashore and send him home. Now everything seemed ready, but there were fresh delays because the governor of Cadiz demanded that a Spanish fleet lying ready in the roads must sail first, and they had to wait a whole fortnight because of this.

Finally, on May 24 they cast anchor again off Santa Cruz, and Leyel hoped that he had seen the last of all his difficulties. But it was to be almost a whole year before he could continue his voyage.

They had hardly reached harbour before they ran into a host of new problems. Only a week after they had cast anchor Jørgen Hansen had gone ashore with a boat to fetch some of the goods they had deposited when he was stopped by some Basques who demanded that the Danish boat row them out to their frigate. Jørgen Hansen could not see that he had any obligation to obey this order so he refused. A couple of hours later the same Basques met Jørgen Hansen when he was alone and attacked him. It was a fierce fight in which they used both stones and daggers. But Hansen was a tough proposition; when the fight became nasty he drew his knife and killed the most violent of the men, the one who had started the fight and gave one of the others a serious wound. He himself received a hard blow to the mouth which cost him a couple of teeth, besides a violent blow to the chest which probably broke some of his ribs; in any case he was spitting blood for several days afterwards.

Leyel had been in the interior, in La Laguna when this happened. But as soon as they heard the news the authorities demanded that he hand over Jørgen Hansen so they could start proceedings against him. However, Leyel realized that if he did so he would never see his good captain again and refused point blank. It was the Basques who had attacked his captain and the latter had only acted in self-defence. The Spaniards accordingly took Leyel and nine of his men and put them in prison. Here they sat for four weeks, and the men received unprecedented harsh treatment, though they were completely innocent.

Finally Leyel was set free. The sources do not allow us to follow all his movements: he was still owed a substantial sum, and from the accounts we can see that he again made several voyages between La Laguna and Santa Cruz, and between Tenerife and the central administration on Gran Canaria. It was again with difficulty that he found a licentiate who tried to see the Danes get justice before the Audiencia on Gran Canaria. But Don Luis managed to have the lawyer dismissed, upon which the man determined to go to Madrid, partly to complain of Don Luis, partly to try to force him to pay Leyel what was owed. Leyel furnished him with a letter to Eiler Ulfeldt asking the latter to assist the lawyer.

By now Leyel felt that he should not wait any longer – each day cost money. It would be better to accept the sum of 12,600 reals the Spaniards were willing to pay.

Though everything might now seem to be in order, Leyel was not to escape from the island without a last drama. This began with a mere routine inspection of the merchant Peter Lützen's accounts. He discovered that Lützen had not entered some money he had received from Captain Jørgen Hansen in August 1640 and in February–March 1642, a sum of 302 pieces-of-eight in all. Lützen had no satisfactory explanation. He seemed wilfully to have swindled the Company, and Leyel gave him a dressing-down.

He must have been pretty rough with him for that evening when Leyel was sitting in his room ashore relaxing with a couple of English merchants over a bottle of canary Lützen came to justify himself. It was only too evident that he was rather drunk, so that when Leyel tried to calm him by asking him to come in the next day and explain matters, the man flew into a passion and shouted that his accounts were quite in order, that he did not think much of Leyel, and the commander should not try to teach him how to keep his accounts. Leyel tried to calm him down and suggested once more that they could discuss the matter peaceably the following day; but right now he wished to talk to his English friends.

But Lützen refused to leave. He kept on grumbling about the way he had been treated. By this time Leyel was tired of him and called for two of his men to help the fellow to leave. He seized a candle so he could light them down the stairs. All should now have been well, but Lützen suddenly turned around, drew a small English pistol from his pocket and fired at Leyel. Fortunately the pistol misfired. At that moment Lützen tore himself loose and ran down the stairs, but suddenly he turned and fired again. Incredibly the pistol misfired a second time. He then ran out through the door and fired a third shot at Leyel, who had run after him. This time the bullet passed between the two seamen and buried itself in the wall not far from Leyel's head. Lützen now took to his heels closely pursued by the seamen. He attempted to slip into a Catholic church, but the door was locked. He was then overpowered, the pistol taken from him, and he was taken on board the *Christianshavn* where he was put under arrest.

All his life Leyel treasured the bullet that had so nearly cost him his life.

A few days later, on March 2, 1643, almost exactly three years after they had sought refuge from the storm at Tenerife they could at last leave the island. The ship's council was summoned to judge Lützen's case. An attempt to murder the commander would normally have led to a death sentence; and it is incredible that Lützen could avoid this fate. But it is plain that the council agreed to overlook the matter and he was instead set ashore on the island of Mayo, one of the Cape Verde Islands. During the examination of him it appeared that he had a somewhat unsavoury past, having brought shame on an honest gentleman's daughter in Norway by telling a lie. When the lie had been discovered he had been fined three marks, upon which he had gone to Denmark where nobody knew his past.

In spite of the lenient sentence Lützen tried to revenge himself on Leyel. In a letter dated April 17, of which he sent copies to both the Danish governor of the Company at Tranquebar, Berent Pessart, and to Claus Rytter, he maintained that he had been unjustly turned off the ship by main force, and that Leyel had completely given up any thought of completing his voyage and had instead gone pirating with an English captain Roberto Blanco, whose real name was probably Robert White.

The sources have nothing to say about Leyel's course after leaving the Cape Verde Islands, but the *Christianshavn* must have continued its lonely voyage to the south. As they got farther south new species of birds appeared. The albatross glided past on its enormously broad wings, and in bad weather the stormy petrels kept them company. They glided so low over the smooth water left in the wake of the ship that it looked as if they were walking on the water. The Spaniards called the bird a petrel in memory of St Peter who had tried to walk on the waters of Lake Genesareth. One day black ravens with white bills appeared, and old seamen assured the men that this was a sure sign that the Cape of Good Hope was not far off. And soon afterwards the *Christianshavn* could drop anchor in the bay near Table Mountain.

It was the custom to stay here a while to cleanse the bottom of the ship and procure fresh supplies of water and firewood. As yet there were no European settlements, so there was probably not much in the way of fresh supplies, but one could often catch a quantity of fish in the bay, and sometimes it was possible to buy cattle from the Hottentots – according to Jon Olafsson the price of a cow was a third of an iron hoop.

It is possible that Leyel, to save time, steered a straight course across the Indian Ocean for the southern tip of India. But the usual route would have taken him to the north, first to Madagascar, where a fresh stop was often made, and then on to the Seychelles and the Comoro Islands making for Socotra off the Horn of Africa. Then across the sea to the Indian coast and not until then could a course be set for Cape Comorin and then again north along the eastern coast of India to Tranquebar.

CHAPTER 6
CLAUS RYTTER AND *THE GILDED SUN*

If Leyel had had a magic mirror in his cabin he could have seen that at about this time Claus Rytter and *The Gilded Sun* were preparing to sail home from Tranquebar. He had completed his voyage without problems, though he had lost twenty of his eighty crewmen before dropping anchor in the road off Tranquebar in early October 1640. But here everything was in hopeless disarray and in a state of decay. Berent Pessart, who had been in charge of the Company's affairs since Roland Crappé had gone home in 1637, had moved his headquarters farther north to Masulipatnam, while the Dutchman Jacob van Stackenborg was left in charge at Tranquebar. Before sailing on Rytter handed over 1000 rigsdaler to van Stackenborg so that he could give the local dyers and weavers a sum to ensure his being able upon his return to collect a stock of textiles suitable for trade with Java and Macassar. Rytter then sailed north again hoping that Pessart would at least have a return cargo ready for him.

Masulipatnam was the centre of trade in plain cotton goods which were produced round about in the homes of many local weavers. These cottons were in great demand on the Sunda Islands. But in Masulipatnam one could also buy tobacco, iron, steel, indigo, and various precious stones, and in its harbour lay a host of local sampans that had come bringing rice, butter, sugar, wax, honey, lacquer, and silk, all of which were sold in the city's colourful and noisy market.

Upon his arrival Rytter found that here, too, the Company's affairs were in a desperate state. Pessart had amassed an enormous debt, which rumour said was in the neighbourhood of 100,000 rigsdaler; however, the Dutch pointed out that Crappé had already left a debt of 16,000 pagodas when he sailed for home. Rytter found it very difficult to get to the bottom of the matter as the accounts had not been kept properly, and Pessart was not very informative. According to the English many of his men were in prison because of his large debts, and the authorities had even threatened to prevent him from buying food for his family unless he paid up, and this he was unable to do. However, it seemed that he was not the only one with embarrassing debts. The English ambassador dared not venture abroad for fear of his creditors. The return cargo Rytter had hoped to find ready and waiting was nowhere to be seen.

But things were still worse. Even the Danish trading station, which had now for years been a kind of centre for Danish trade in all the East had been lost, as the Golcondian governor had impounded all Danish property as surety for the claims of some Indian merchants on Pessart, and the house was now guarded by the governor's men. On the other hand, the governor sent the usual welcoming presents out to *The Gilded Sun* in the form of goats, bananas, and fresh bread. Rytter, however, felt far from safe and realized that he must be on his guard, or the creditors would impound his ship, his money, and his trading goods. Accordingly he did not dare go ashore, and when asked he declared that the ship was the personal possession of His Majesty, the Danish king, and had nothing whatsoever to do with the East India Company.

As already mentioned, there was both a Dutch and an English trading station in the town, and Pessart craftily managed to obtain some cash by persuading two of his English acquaintances among the merchants to take up a loan of 7000 pagodas at 3½ per cent interest and then give him the money at the rate of 2½ per cent. If these figures are not due to an error in the English source, they must prove that Pessart had great charm and formidable persuasive powers! He used the money to pay off on his huge debt; but for the English it must have been a poor bargain.

As the English furthermore agreed to become surety for him Pessart managed to slip out to *The Gilded Sun*, where Rytter asked him to explain the frightful mess the Company's affairs were in. At Tranquebar Rytter had found Dansborg in a state of decay, apparently no vestige of discipline, the soldiers and chaplains equally drunk, and everything in a complete mess with no sign of leadership or order. He had furthermore been told that Pessart owed the nayak of Tanjore a sum of 12,000 pagodas, an utterly irresponsible action as it might entitle the nayak to throw the Danes out of Tranquebar for defaulting on the treaty. Pessart defended his negligence in this respect saying that he simply had not had the money to pay the annual tribute. He admitted that this was unfortunate; but there had been no ship from home for four years, and all his business deals had fallen through. He also said that the Dutch Company had likewise had to take up big loans, and the shortage of money meant that interest on the loans rose to 24-36 per cent.

A famine in the region had also caused hundreds of weavers and dyers to flee to other parts of the country in the endeavour to find food, so that it had become almost impossible to procure the usual quantities of textiles for trade with the Islands and the prices had risen sky-high.

Rytter must have listened impatiently to Pessart's explanations. He wanted to see a balance sheet for the Company's finances and a report on the trade situation. He had expected to find that Pessart had collected goods for a return cargo so that he could return home immediately. This was to have been Pessart's main task; but the warehouses both at Tranquebar and here in Masulipatnam were empty, and there seemed to remain only a bottomless debt besides the imminent danger of Rytter himself being sent to a debtor's prison because of Pessart's incompetence.

Pessart had to admit that he was not able to offer much in the way of assistance, but all his trading ventures had been dogged by misfortune. Everything he attempted seemed to have miscarried. Several of his English friends thought that he had both acted wisely and had been eager to find new markets, but added that "God had not wished to further his plans". Now he had had to give up the Danish station at Balasore which Crappé had opened.

At one time he had had the good fortune to obtain a large quantity of cloves from Macassar, to which island they had been smuggled in spite of the Dutch efforts to prevent this. He had intended to sell the cloves in Masulipatnam at a huge profit, but the great quantities on the market that year had led to stiff competition with both the Dutch and the English, so that the price had fallen drastically, something the financially sound Dutch and English Companies could manage, but it had completely ruined the Danish Company. Pessart admitted that he had been rash to enter into a trade war with the others, and the competiton had been disastrous. But what was he to do? He had had this large quantity of cloves and they could not just be kept in store indefinitely.

In 1639 the Dutch, English, and Danish agents in Masulipatnam had been ordered to present themselves before the king of Golconda, a difficult journey lasting several days. The king had there informed them that he expected them to present him with a gift of 600,000 pagodas each as the local governor had promised. The Europeans were flabbergasted. Such a sum was out of the question. The well-to-do Dutch coughed up 3000 pagodas and promised to send him an elephant and five Persian horses. The English murmured that at the moment they were unfortunately unable to present the king with any gift worthy of His Majesty. The king was furious and sent his men back with them to the English station where the English were ordered to open all the chests and cupboards and then vacate the premises while the place was ransacked. Rumour had it that the king and 100 of his women examined every nook and corner for

4-6 hours and only found valuables amounting to less than 2000 pagodas. The Danes were even worse off, and when their station was ransacked and nothing of value was found they were let off with the promise to pay 2000 when the next ship from Denmark arrived.

The difficult times had forced Pessart to look for new openings. He had bought diamonds from a mine in Golconda and tried to sell them on Sumatra; he had sent a ship to Persia with spices and sugar and had expected to make a large profit – but it turned out that just that year the goods could not be sold at a profit, and he had only fallen deeper into debt. It was easy enough to blame him for the Company's affairs being in such disorder; he had truly done everything in his power, but it seemed that he was born under an unlucky star. Because he lacked men for one of the small vessels he had recently hired two Portuguese; but they had been discovered making plans to murder the captain and all the other Danes on board and then make off with the ship. This calamity had fortunately been averted, and the Portuguese sent to their punishment in San Thomé.

Since he realized the Company's desperate situation Pessart had even proposed to the Portuguese that they could buy Dansborg, as now that he had moved to Masulipatnam Tranquebar was no longer the centre of the Company's activities. This was probably an arrangement the directors in Copenhagen might find difficult to accept; but in his difficult situation it seemed to him a possible method of raising some money. However, the Portuguese had not accepted the offer, as they were doubtful as to the importance of the fortress. In 1640, when the English were looking for a new base on the Coast of Coromandel their leaders in Surat suggested taking over Tranquebar and Dansborg should the Danes' need for funds force them to sell, but this, too, came to nothing.

Pessart also told of the last big catastrophe, which Rytter probably had not even heard of yet. He had sent the Company's sloop, the *St Jakob*, which had arrived in India in 1636, to Bantam and Macassar with the usual goods, and for once all had gone well. In 1640 the vessel was on its way home with a rich cargo, when a hurricane drove it up into the Bay of Bengal where it was in danger of driving ashore. The crew tried to save it by anchoring off Pipeley; but the cables snapped and they lost both their anchors. They then tried using their guns instead, but these were unable to hold the ship. The storm drove them on to the shore where the vessel was wrecked. It might perhaps have been saved as some Indian captains from Masulipatnam had offered their assistance; but the governor forbade it. Instead he had his tent pitched on the beach so that he could enjoy the awesome scene. The ship was then broken up by the waves; the governor laid his hands on everything that could be saved, twenty-seven men drowned, and the surviving sailors were lodged in a house where they soon became so ill that they felt sure there had been poison in their food. In any case sixteen Danes died in the course of the next three days. We lack information as to what happened to those still alive. We only know that the captain Nicolaj Samson escaped and reached Tranquebar in safety. Pessart put the value of the ship's cargo at 150,000 rigsdaler, while the vessel itself with its guns might add another 25,000. Besides this, there was on board a high-ranking Muslim mullah, Mornin, who was on a pilgrimage to Mecca at the head of a group of fifty people. They claimed to have had with them property to the value of 70,000 rigsdaler, and the Sultan of Macassar now demanded this sum of the Danish company.

It was a paralyzing blow for the Company, and it was this news that had made Pessart's creditors in Masulipatnam demand that he be put in jail.

Pessart also said that he had had stiff competition everywhere from the Dutch. Even the Portuguese, who had now had colonies for more than one hundred years in India and in Ceylon, had seen the Dutch infringe more and more on their old monopoly. Both nations wanted to control the million pounds of cinnamon produced in Ceylon every year, and the following years were to see a nearly continuous struggle for mastery, which only ended with the final Dutch conquest of the island in 1656.

Pessart never produced the desired papers and accounts, and Rytter ends his report by writing that he has had no assistance whatsoever, either in word or deed, from Berent Pessart.

As matters stood Rytter thought that he could best serve the Company's interests by trading on his own and using *The Gilded Sun* according to the usual scheme of buying textiles along the Coast of Coromandel, sailing them over to the trading posts in Bantam and Macassar, where they could be sold at a handsome profit, and then buying cloves, sugar, and porcelain, silk, etc., there. Before leaving he took stock of his assets: 27,000 rigsdaler in ready money, some cloth he reckoned might be sold for another 1000 rigsdaler, and a quantity of lead perhaps worth 6000 rigsdaler, besides a number of long muskets and gilt mirrors to be used as presents for the rajahs.

So he left Masulipatnam only a week after he had arrived and sailed on to the north. Six weeks later he was back. Masulipatnam was the best trading post on the whole eastern coast for cotton goods, and Rytter had discovered how difficult it was elsewhere to obtain a stock of these goods to use for bartering on the Sunda Islands. He then risked returning trusting that the authorities had accepted his former assurances that his ship was the personal property of the Danish king and had no connection whatsoever with the Danish East India Company.

But this time his assurances did not help, though he thought he had taken every precaution. As he later wrote to his "good friend and trusted brother" Willem Leyel, he had sent the capable Herman Clausen Rugmand ahead to obtain "guarantees in writing that we might freely come to Masulipatnam without let or hindrance to trade there, and that none of the Company's creditors or any other person whatsoever would exclude us or His Majesty's goods from the market". Herman Clausen had then returned with the desired written assurances, and relying on these Rytter entered the town with some of his men on November 5, rented a house as a base for the new royal trade, which he persisted in maintaining had nothing to do with the Danish Company, took 8000 pieces-of-eight ashore with him and began buying the usual cotton goods. However, the Moors did not believe his assurances and kept a suspicious eye on all his dealings. For a while all was well. But in spite of all their promises the Moors who were owed money by the Company demanded that Rytter pay off on the Company's debts. They simply did not believe his explanations. He flew the same red-and-white flag that had earlier flown over the trading station, so the two must belong to the same nation. Rytter tried once more to maintain that the goods he had on board did not belong to the Company, but were the personal property of the Danish king, and when they refused to believe him he summoned the local English and Dutch merchants and had them read the – presumably carefully selected – documents he had on board. But to no avail.

On December 19, 1640, he was imprisoned in the same debtors' prison as Pessart, together with two of his men. About his stay there he writes that in order to obtain a little warmth in the chilly nights he had to give the Indian soldiers, who guarded him and his two companions, money for firewood for the night, and for betel and tobacco. However, he seems speedily to have regained his freedom, as he enters a sum paid to the men who carried him back to Masulipatnam in a palanquin. But on December 26 he was again imprisoned, though only a dozen days later he was released by the governor and allowed to return to his house because he was ill. But as soon as he was on his feet again he was taken back to the prison on January 13, 1641. And here he had to remain for five days.

But it could not go on like this. While he was held in helpless captivity the monsoon would soon blow itself out, and in that case he would have to wait nearly a year before he could sail to Java and Celebes as he had intended. So he apparently agreed to pay 5000 pagodas as an instalment on Pessart's debts, as well as 1000 pagodas and ten pieces of red cloth as a present to the viceroy. He also had to agree to pay the rest of the debt over the next three years. He was then allowed to return to his house and begin to buy cotton cloth as he had intended. But it is worth noting that in the long run Rytter got his own back. When at a later period his ship was anchored in the roads off Masulipatnam he seized one of the viceroy's ships there and helped himself to compensation for the 1000 pagodas and ten pieces of red cloth. How relations between them were after that is anybody's guess.

Rytter closes his letter to Leyel: "Now after this brief account I wish to warn my good friend not to believe any Moor's firman or letter, for they are all lies, and they do not keep their promises. Beware of Pessart – he is not to be trusted. Beware of fair words. May God send you better fortune than I have had."

Now that Rytter finally had his freedom he unloaded and sold the lead which had lain as ballast in the bottom of the ship, bought up a store of the various cotton goods he knew were most coveted on the Islands and then steered a course for Tranquebar to fetch the textiles he hoped lay ready for him there and to hear if there was any news of Leyel. It was now eighteen months since they had been separated off Tenerife and he had heard nothing since.

In September 1641 Rytter was back in Tranquebar where he was given the news that the Company had suffered yet another disaster. The sloop *Charitas* which had been used in the local trade had been to Pipeley at the northern end of the Bay of Bengal to buy rice and sugar, but on its way southwards a storm had driven it ashore where it was wrecked, two Danes and five Indians drowned.

The Gilded Sun left Tranquebar on September 21 and continued on its way to Bantam where the cotton goods were sold. However, the English reported triumphantly that Rytter had only made a profit of 50 per cent, whereas the English had made 100 per cent. Rytter bought the usual return goods: sugar, cloves, etc., and sailed back to Masulipatnam to sell them.

The Dutch were steadily gaining ground. In January 1641 they seized Malacca from the Portuguese. And Rytter discovered that in competition with them the Danes would always come off second best. They made him feel that they despised the somewhat clumsy Dane who was encroaching on their territory, they considered him a newcomer who knew little about trade. Rytter tried to avenge himself for their taunts by telling them that the Danes would soon oust them from the Islands. He boasted that five large ships were on their way from Denmark with rich cargoes and when they arrived the Danes would no longer pay customs to the Dutch while the high and mighty Dutch would have to pay a large duty when they came to Tranquebar. The Dutch laughed behind his back and murmured that he must have a very lively imagination. The English also spoke condescendingly of the Danish trade as "a poore fainte trade, not worth mentioning".

The constant loss of men from the *Sun*'s crew forced Rytter to take on twenty-one "black" sailors. His accounts give us a glimpse of the life and requirements on board. Every ship carried a store of the things the sailors needed, and meticulous accounts were kept of everything handed out to them. Each man had his own page in the ledger; for instance we can see that in 1641 Rasmus Nielsen from the town of Guldborg received six linen nightcaps at 2 shillings each. In the roads off Masulipatnam he received three shirts for which he had to pay 1 rigsdaler and 19½ shillings. In 1642 he received one piece of Bengali cotton cloth and later in Tranquebar 8 pagodas in cash. Later that year in Bantam he received 1 rigsdaler for an old woman in that city, apparently because he had been ill and she had nursed him, for a little later she is paid another rigsdaler for medicine. He must then have recovered his health for in 1643 when on board again he receives another piece of cotton cloth and later two pieces of Masulipatnam sailcloth, for which he is charged 3 ort, and again three shirts for 1 rigsdaler and 2 ort.

Pessart, too, resumed his trade. On January 18, 1642, he appointed Nicolaj Samson captain of the *Fortuna* and ordered him to make the usual voyage to Macassar. Samson left soon after. At this time the English had established themselves in Madras, thinking that they could make a handsome profit by buying betelnuts in Tranquebar and selling them farther up the coast. For this reason the English agent Francis Day came to Tranquebar where he bought a large stock of nuts at his own expense. He also seems to have lent Pessart 1000 reals, though as someone tartly remarked "it is hardly likely that he will repay the loan". However, Day seems to have taken Samson's wife, servants, and jewels as a kind of security and had them all taken to Madras where they had to remain for the time being. The other Englishmen remarked that a private showdown between Day and Samson could hardly be avoided when Samson came home.

Rytter still did not have goods enough for a return cargo and now sailed north and south along the coast where he bought fresh stores of cotton cloth. From his accounts we can see that in December he bought in Narsepur 54½ maen (1 maen was 37.5 kilos) of gunpowder from a Moor "because part of our own powder was in a bad state, and in Bantam I had had to present the king with 4 barrels and some cannon-balls if I was to expect any help from him and he would not listen to excuses". On February 23 he again left Tranquebar and made for Bantam accompanied by the English vessel *The Diamond* whose crew he had to assist on the voyage because they ran short of provisions, the voyage being more difficult than either of them had anticipated. The two ships were forced to go in to Celebaer on Sumatra to get water, and not until June 16 did they finally reach Bantam after almost four months at sea, during which they had suffered greatly from thirst. By then the *Sun* was in poor shape.

On board his ship Rytter had a man called Anders Nielsen, who had been employed as a merchant by Pessart at Masulipatnam; but Nielsen did not care much for Pessart and his drunken friends. So Rytter gave him the job of merchant on the *Sun* and left Herman Clausen in Bantam to establish a Danish trading post and manage things there. In Bantam Rytter also had to find a new mate and some seamen for the voyage home "as our men have almost all died". It was a constant problem to find suitable men. But fortunately the president of the English station in Bantam managed to find him several able Englishmen and a number of others. Rytter also bought medicines off an English barber as the medicine chest on board the *Sun* was empty.

With a good load of spices and other goods from the Sunda Islands, besides a quantity of pepper and ginger from Tranquebar, Rytter felt that he was at last in possession of an acceptable return cargo for Denmark.

Everything was now loaded and packed carefully for the long voyage home. His cargo consisted of, among other things, 678 bar of pepper, 5000 rigsdaler worth of sugar, a quantity of ginger and cloves, though not nearly as much as he had hoped for, some sapanwood for the dyeing trade, some silks, damask, and satin, and finally some diamonds and other precious stones.

In Tranquebar he again received bad news. A report had come in about the Danish station at Pipeley. It was run by the merchant Poul Nielsen, another merchant, some assistants, and a few other Danes, besides some Indian shop assistants, and a small force of Indian soldiers from Tranquebar, who were meant to protect the station from thieves.

The local Indian governor Mirza Mumin had made such exorbitant demands that no man on earth could satisfy him. Whenever the Danes had made a good bargain he would turn up with excessive demands, and he kept coming up with new taxes. Besides this the Danes found it increasingly difficult to collect their outstanding claims on the local merchants. Since every other attempt had failed with an especially notorious Persian, who in spite of repeated requests had refused to pay his debts, the Danes decided to take him prisoner in his own house. However, the Persian escaped, so Poul Nielsen had sent armed men around the town to find him, and when they did not succeed they took one of his slave girls and some of his goods into custody at the Danish trading post. But the Indians could not accept the Danes taking the law into their own hands, and a force of 300 men of the Great Mogul's troops was sent against them, the trading station was taken and burned to the ground. The Danes were taken prisoner, chained, and sent to another town. All the Company's goods in the place were impounded. After some time Poul Nielsen and some of the others succeeded in escaping, and in the course of the next summer they made their way down to Tranquebar.

Rytter had hoped that when he got to Tranquebar he would find that Leyel had arrived with the *Christianshavn*. It was now known that the Spaniards had delayed him on Tenerife and that he had had a difficult time, though nobody could say with any certainty when he would arrive.

But Rytter felt that he could not stay any longer – his ship must leave for home, and the sooner the better. It was now three and a half years since he had left Copenhagen. The last goods were brought on board, the guns on *The Gilded Sun* thundered across the water as a last greeting, and the guns on Dansborg's walls replied. Soon the big Danish flag on the tower disappeared in the haze. It was March 16, 1643 – only a fortnight after Leyel had finally left Tenerife.

After crossing the Indian Ocean Rytter stopped at Christiansbaij on Madagascar, where he arrived on May 27. Here they stayed for five months to wait until the winter and the worst storms at the Cape were over. He also had to obtain fresh provisions, as an inspection of the casks showed that all the salt meat they had brought with them from home was rotten. They had to throw it all overboard and try to replenish their stocks on the island.

Soon after the ship had anchored, the local king came down to the beach with his women and children. Rytter gave him a hearty reception and showered him with gifts, for, as he wrote, he did this so "that I might win his friendship and we might be safe in his country and suffer no evil from his people and I might buy cattle, rice, and other necessaries". Besides a gift of 20 rigsdaler in ready money he gave him two large porcelain bowls, a mirror, 4 yards of red cloth, a large Bengali tobacco pipe, ½ picol of sugar (1 picol was about 60 kilograms), another little sack of sugar, and for the king's wife a tobacco pipe of mother-of-pearl. The king's mother was also given tobacco worth 1 rigsdaler, two of his small children ½ rigsdaler each, and the king's slave who served as interpreter received a couple of shillings.

About a month later Rytter visited the king who presented him with five bullocks, besides a quantity of rice and potatoes. They were also able to buy other provisions, including 1200 lemons for the men.

While the Danes lay in this bay some Frenchmen suddenly appeared. They said that their ship was anchored at a little distance in the Santa Lucia Bay. Their captain Rossemont asked for several things they lacked, which Rytter gave them, as well as some gifts: ½ picol of sugar, a small sack of pepper, a pot of ginger, and a couple of Taiwanese silk stockings. Later Rytter sent his second merchant David Leyel, one of Leyel's relatives, to the French to ask for rice and other things he lacked. Europeans were all usually very willing to help each other when they met on foreign shores, and Rytter received a large quantity of very fine white rice, for which he paid 135 rigsdaler; the French also gave the Danes a number of things they needed, such as a large copper pot, a cask of French wine, a quantity of nails, five barrels of salt, a barrel of resin and four bullocks.

Whenever the ship lay at anchor there was always the danger that the men would run away. It also happened here, and Rytter sent David Leyel off into the country with one of the Frenchmen in an effort to track down some of them. Meanwhile the cooper was busy repairing the water casks, but Rytter was discouraged by the result. Water was the most important of all the supplies on board. If the barrels were leaky it could lead to a catastrophe at sea, and Rytter wrote of them: "they are not worth much, and [we] do not know how they will keep on the voyage".

In late October *The Gilded Sun* again weighed anchor and sailed safely around the Cape of Good Hope. By March 1644 the ship had reached Pernambuco in Brazil. Rytter went ashore for three days with both merchants and Willem Leyel's son, young Hans Leyel, to answer the governor's usual questions as to what ship it was and where they were going. Rytter asked for permission to buy the provisions he needed. During their stay the four men spent 106 guilders for food, beer, wine, etc. (One guilder seems to have been about 3/8 rigsdaler.) Among the larger items he mentions 788 litres of Madeira wine for 334 guilders, and 5 casks of beef for 490 guilders. Also 2 casks of pork, 1751 pounds of bread, an anchor for 395 guilders, and an anchor cable, in all their expenses were 3500 rigsdaler. On May 12 the ship left and sailed on across the Atlantic and south around England. All on board heaved a sigh of relief at being once more in European waters. Now they would soon be home again after an absence of four and a half years.

They received a warm welcome from the first ships they encountered, a couple of English warships, which sold them some provisions they badly needed. But soon afterwards the leaky old ship got into difficulties in Tor Bay. Fortunately, help was at hand. A kind English captain Boon sent a pilot over to them from his ship and towed them into Portsmouth, where they anchored in late July.

So far all seemed well. But Rytter was unfortunate enough to land in the middle of an ongoing dispute between Christian IV and the English Parliament. A civil war had broken out in England where many could no longer tolerate Charles I's highhanded disregard of the rights of Parliament. He had ruled for eleven years without summoning a parliament, and now his subjects rebelled. In 1643 King Christian had – partly from family feeling as Charles was the son of Christian IV's sister Anne and partly to uphold the rights of the Crown – sent a ship *The Ark* with a load of ammunition to Charles. But the ship had been seized by Parliament's naval forces and confiscated. Furious at this treatment Christian had seized English ships and goods in the Sound and in Glückstadt and had the captains imprisoned in Copenhagen, which naturally made Parliament furious.

So that when Rytter and *The Gilded Sun* unsuspectingly arrived at Portsmouth Parliament thought it a heaven-sent opportunity to obtain security in the Danish assets and thus force Christian to release the ships he had seized.

Only a fortnight after he had arrived at Portsmouth Rytter notes in his account book the sum which he, who evidently did not know enough English to understand official documents, had had to pay "to have translated Parliament's arrest of our ship by the ordinance they have passed of how they mean to deal with our ship while it is in Portsmouth".

In September Parliament sent two emissaries to the Danish king in an endeavour to come to an agreement. They deplored that, because of complaints from the injured English captains, Parliament had been forced to detain *The Gilded Sun*; however, the captain was still in possession of his ship, and they had appointed representatives both of Parliament and the merchants concerned to see that nothing was removed from the ship. They promised that the ship would immediately be released as soon as their differences were resolved.

The negotiations with the English emissaries ended with the agreement that King Christian would pay the English merchants damages amounting to 174,000 rigsdaler. *The Gilded Sun* was to count for 74,000 rigsdaler, but the ship and its goods were to be sold and the cost of the sale be paid by the Danes. This latter sum amounted to 13,969 rigsdaler. On June 3 Christian signed a bond for 100,000 rigsdaler and promised furthermore to pay the remaining 13,969 rigsdaler. But this sum was probably never paid – the Exchequer was empty.

During these lengthy negotiations Claus Rytter was stranded in London. There were lots of difficulties. To cover his expenses he had to borrow money from the large trading company, The Merchant Adventurers, and others, and he writes that one day in January 1646 "I was arrested in the Exchange in London by Paul Richards, James Feiff, John Thomasson Hamborger and Carlos Blood for the wages due them from His Majesty in Denmark for their voyage from India with the ship, the 'Sun', as they had been hired in India when we lacked men, and since both ship and goods had been sequestrated they had appealed to the Admiralty Court. I was to find security or go to prison".

It seems it was no easy task to captain ships belonging to the East India Company at this time – Rytter was now for the second time on this voyage threatened with a debtor's prison. To get out of this new difficulty he had to engage a lawyer to aid him in court where he was sentenced to pay the seamen their wages, a sum of 35 pounds sterling, 7 shillings, and 8 pence.

On April 30 the Danish authorities wrote to Claus Rytter regarding *The Gilded Sun*: "What has been decided with the English Parliamentary emissaries can be seen from the enclosed abstract. He must follow these instructions, but above all look after the King's interests and see that the goods are sold at as good a price as possible."

Finally, everything was settled. All the goods and the ship were sold, and Rytter was free to return to Denmark. But here he ran into fresh difficulties. Once at home in the offices of the East India Company in Copenhagen he submitted his accounts which showed that with an initial capital of 22,962 rigsdaler in ready money and lead he had made a profit of 30,940 rigsdaler – not an impressive result, but not bad considering the difficulties he had encountered. But when the Company's directors had the treasurer Peter Vibe check the account books he thought that Rytter had charged too much for provisions both in Brazil and in England. Rytter defended himself claiming that the expenses were not larger than necessary, for one had to remember that all his stocks had been used up on the long voyage, and that prices in Brazil were very high, because nothing was to be had but what had been brought from the Netherlands, and the Dutch naturally refused to sell their goods without a large profit.

Another thing criticized by Peter Vibe was that while in the East Rytter had spent lavishly and given several wholly unnecessary and very expensive gifts. The same criticism that had been directed at Roland Crappé who had claimed that in the East it was essential to give generous gifts in order to establish good relations and that it often paid. Rytter claimed that by giving suitable presents he had been exempt from paying customs at Macassar, both on imports and exports, and the customs at Macassar were 7 per cent both on arrival and departure. So that by this means considerable sums of money had been saved. An example of such a present, which is almost in the nature of a bribe, is entered on December 18, 1642, while *The Gilded Sun* lay in the roads before Bantam. Rytter had paid some influential persons 60 rigsdaler, for them to obtain a promise "from both the kings in Bantam that the English were not to be allowed to buy any pepper until we had completed our cargo".

Among the lesser expenses, Rytter had an entry dated September 20, 1640, the day before the *Sun* left Tranquebar for Masulipatnam of 6 rigsdaler: "Given to our white and black soldiers in the fortress for arrack". Likewise on February 22, 1642, on leaving Tranquebar for the Islands there is an entry of 10 rigsdaler given to "the white and black soldiers as a present when I went on board the ship before sailing to encourage them to do their duty". On Christmas Day he gave alms of 6 fano to the poor which was carefully entered in the expense account. And when the *Sun* was to leave Bantam there is an entry: "Gave the blacks who were to stay in the trading post under Herman Clausen a present of 12 rigsdaler to encourage them in their duty".

However, it was hardly these repeated gifts to the people employed by the Company that irritated the directors in Copenhagen, but the often very expensive "gifts" that were customary in the East if one was to do business. The custom in these countries was very different from what it was at home, and Rytter had a difficult time trying to explain this to the directors. In his defence he wrote: "The presents I have given in India from the goods given to me for that purpose were never given unless it was absolutely necessary. Or they were the goods that were most serviceable and could be had locally at the least expense, for according to the custom of these countries nobody can obtain an audience of the king or his officials, and nothing can be done without presenting gifts, nor have I done His Majesty any harm by following this practice. For by such gifts I have obtained free and reliable negotiations, for instance in Bantam I was exempt from paying customs or any other fee, which, if I had had to pay these would have meant a load of difficulties in the customs houses as you can imagine, and this was all done away with by this means."

It was sometimes quite large sums that were used in this manner; thus he notes on February 22, 1642: "Gave Stackenborg for a present to Tipo Nayak 400 rigsdaler, and 1 gold chain worth 364 rigsdaler. Also 1 small gold chain for Almo Nayak in Tranquebar worth 21 rigsdaler."

CHAPTER 7
LEYEL ARRIVES

The Great Mogul, ruler over all of northern India, was at this time
Shah Jahan, the man who built the fabulously beautiful Taj Mahal, and
whose riches were legendary. Rumour had it that on the anniversary of
his accession to the throne he not only kept the custom of having his
own weight in gold and jewels distributed among the people, but also
had pots of precious stones and jewels poured over his head as a method
of averting misfortune, whereupon he let the treasure be distributed
among the spectators. The value of these gifts was estimated at as much
as £1,600,000. His huge kingdom stretched all the way down the Deccan peninsula to the river Godaveri. Masulipatnam did not belong to
him, but to the kingdom of Golconda, while Tanjore was a more or less
independent state.

The miserable financial problems and the many calamities had made
Pessart desperate. The unjust treatment of the Danish trading station
at Pipeley and the lack of assistance when the *St Jakob* was in danger,
besides the seizure of its valuable cargo, had ruined the Company's
finances to such a degree that extreme measures were called for. He
seems to have bought a new ship which he had called the *Valby*. If the
Bengalis would not trade with him as honest folk and adhere to the
most elementary rules of trade they should be paid back in their own
coin. So in late 1642 he declared war on the Mogul, furnished his two
sloops, the *Fortuna* and the *Valby*, with cannon and crew, and sent them
off as privateers on the lookout for Bengali prizes. In this way he hoped
to recoup all his losses.

If anybody ventured to warn him against following such a course he
probably shrugged his shoulders and asked if they did not know the old
saying: "God created the rabbit and the Bengali". The risk was not so
great when the ships were armed with European guns.

As early as the end of 1642 the two Danish privateers seized a fairly
large vessel from the Great Mogul. It was brought in to Tranquebar,
where the goods were sold at a handsome profit. The vessel itself was
incorporated in the little Danish fleet with the name *The Bengali Prize*,
was armed with guns from Dansborg and sailed for a number of years in
the service of the Danish Company.

One source of information from this period is the Dutch Dagh Register, which consists of reports to the Dutch East India Company's headquarters at Batavia from the various Dutch trading stations in the whole district regarding both the Dutch trade and that of their rivals, news of the arrival and departure of the ships, and everything thought to be of any interest to the directors. According to this Pessart escaped from his above-mentioned imprisonment on January 10, 1643, and sailed with the *Fortuna* to Tranquebar. From here he wrote a letter to the governor of Masulipatnam making fun of the debtors he had left behind.

A little later there was news that Leyel had sailed from the Canary Islands in March and could thus soon be expected at Tranquebar. Pessart was not very keen on meeting him and hastened the work on his three ships, the sloop *Valby*, *The Bengali Prize*, and a two-masted barge, and sent off two other vessels to trade at Bantam and Macassar.

Before he could sail himself the garrison at Dansborg was awakened at dawn on September 5, 1643, by the sound of gunshots and trumpets from the sea, and soon they were able to recognize the *Christianshavn*.

Pessart was presumably far from overjoyed and probably swore at his continuing bad luck. If only he had sailed a few days earlier. He reluctantly gave orders to raise the Danish flag on Dansborg's tall flagstaff and shoot the usual Danish signal of nine shots from the great guns. Now he would have to face it out and then see how he could escape from Leyel. He had no wish to listen to his questions and everlasting reproaches as to the state of the Company's affairs. Pessart fully realized that the station was practically bankrupt, and the drunken chaplain Niels Andersen from the village of Udbyneder in Jutland was likewise nervous about the new situation. Leyel was presumably known as a strict master, a stickler for order. He would not approve of drinking and inefficiency, and many of the men must have dreaded his coming. The other chaplain, Christen Pedersen Storm, had already been put in prison by Rytter because of his drunkenness and violent conduct. Nor could Leyel expect much help from the old bedridden merchant Jacob van Stackenborg.

Leyel told of his voyage. After the ship had at last left the Canary Islands all had gone well. He had only lost two men, a result he had every right to be proud of. Leyel must have asked how Claus Rytter had managed, whether he had obtained a suitable return cargo and when he had left. Like Rytter he must have asked to see the Company's accounts and whether the annual payment to the nayak of Tanjore had been made.

Nobody knows what Pessart answered to such questions, but it seems that it was some time before Leyel heard that the tribute to the nayak had not been paid for a number of years.

Leyel must have been immensely relieved to have reached his destination after the many frustrations and the years he had wasted because of Don Luis Fernandez de Cordoba. But he must have realized from the beginning that a host of new problems awaited him in India. Pessart did not seem equal to the task of managing the Company's affairs.

The fortress of Dansborg was now complete. In the middle was a square courtyard for drilling the soldiers, surrounded by buildings on all four sides. These were again surrounded by thick ramparts with bastions in the four corners. On top of each bastion was a sentry-box where the soldiers kept guard. Here they were protected from the burning sun in the daytime and kept at least partly dry during the tropical rains. On top of each sentry-box was a dome of stone and a small tower with a gilt vane on top. Around the fort the water shimmered in a moat formed by water from the river Wadiaru. Access to the fort was gained from the north where a drawbridge led from the town across the moat and on through a winding gate which prevented enemies from shooting directly into the courtyard. A guard was naturally always posted outside the gate. A smaller gate, the water-gate, is also mentioned, which opened right onto the beach and made it easy to load and unload the ships.

On the east side of the courtyard stood a tall building, the ground floor of which was used as a warehouse, but above this were lodgings for the commandant, the chief merchant, and the chaplain, as well as a dining hall for festive occasions. Here one also found the council room, the court, and the clerk's office. On the roof was a tall tower with a weather vane and a flagstaff from which a huge Danish flag flew. In the beginning the church had stood in the middle of the courtyard, but this had been demolished, and a new church installed in the tall building on the east side.

The northern and western wings contained the soldiers' living quarters, and towards the south was a stone well near the large kitchen with its open fireplaces, and store rooms for rice, flour, wine casks, etc. On the ramparts stood some eighty or ninety iron guns of varying sizes. The largest had a range of 800-900 metres, the smaller ones only about half this. The fortress also had a good supply of muskets. So, by and large, Dansborg was a fortress that could easily compare with other European fortresses on the Coast – and it is still there, though the sea

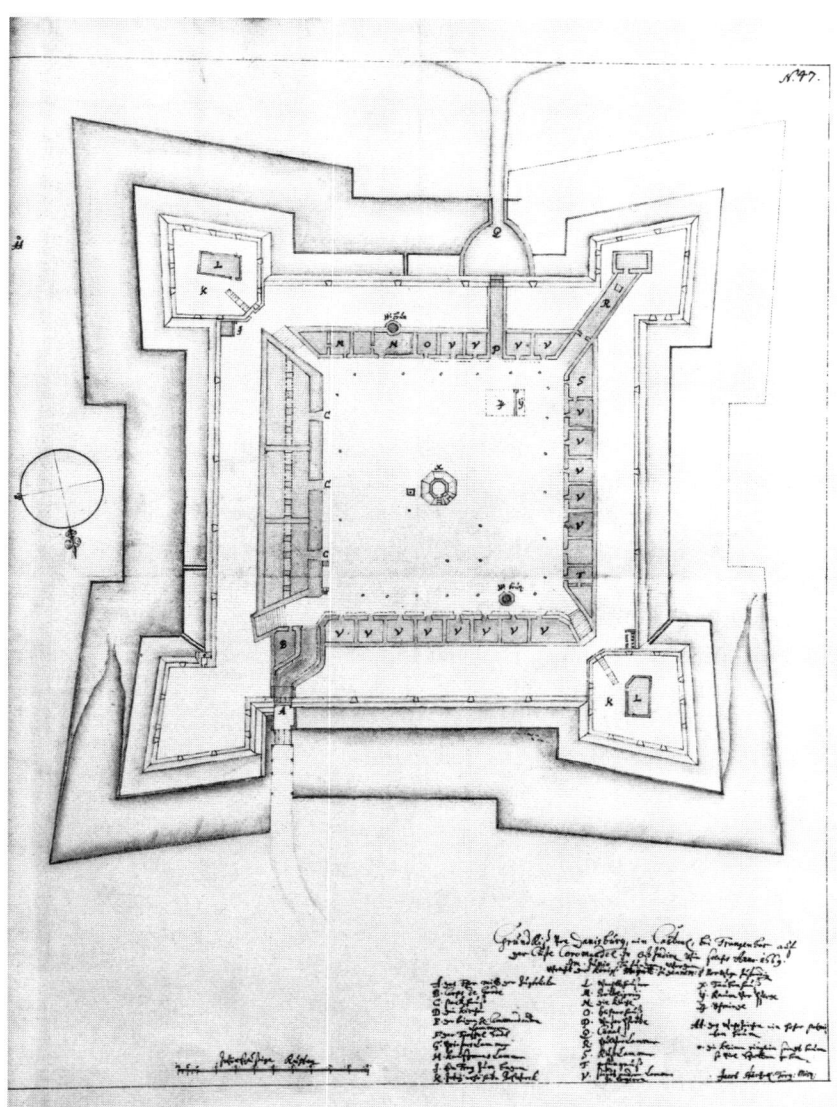

Ground plan of Ove Gjedde's fortress Dansborg 1669. A is the gate with the draw-bridge, C the warehouses; above these the church, the commander's apartments and the dining hall. N is the kitchen, and to the south at P the watergate. (Frederik V's Atlas, no. 48. The Royal Library.)

is gradually eating away at the shore. However, the decay is everywhere clearly visible.

Towards the sea was a yellow sandy beach with the fishermen's small boats drawn up on the sands. Jon Olafsson describes the beach as being so beautiful that "when one walks towards the sun every second grain of sand seems to be of the purest gold, and every other of silver". Behind the fortress lay the small town of Tranquebar with its temple towers. The name of the town in the local language, Tamil, was Tarangambadi, which means something like "the town near the surf", or, more poetically, "the town near the singing waves". Few Danes probably made the effort to learn Tamil, but, on the other hand, quite a few of the inhabitants learned enough Danish to manage. Thus, a Niels Kiöping, who visited Tranquebar thirty years after Dansborg was built, writes: "there were Negroes who spoke excellent Danish".

Without irrigation the soil was barren. There was no rain most of the year, and the only plants were prickly pears with their long sharp thorns and beautiful yellow blossoms, a few thorny bushes and some palm trees. This wild land was home to jackals and snakes.

Even Leyel's first glimpse of the fortress showed him the decay that had set in. In a report he sent home he says that the ramparts were in a miserable state, large portions had crumbled away, the moats were half filled in with rubble. It was evident that the drawbridge could no longer be raised, the woodwork had been eaten by the white ants, and all the buildings were badly neglected. It was all even worse than he had feared. Pessart was plainly a drunkard and incompetent.

One of Pessart's excuses for the decay so visible everywhere about the fortress must have been that Dansborg was no longer of much use. It was not the right place to trade. The cotton goods that had gradually become the main articles of trade had to be purchased farther north. Even Roland Crappé, on his last voyage, had made Masulipatnam the centre for the Company's trade. It was there Pessart had his headquarters, and, as already mentioned, he was in favour of selling or abandoning Dansborg. It served no purpose to waste money and effort there. So it had been his intention to sail north as soon as possible with the ships that were almost fully loaded. It was that time of year when it was necessary to bring the ships up to safe harbours before the October storms broke loose and no ship could survive on the open road off Tranquebar.

As to the empty warehouses, he could explain that he had already sent two ships with good loads off to the Islands, and now his own ships had also been loaded. Besides, Claus Rytter had also emptied the warehouses to get a load for the *Sun* before setting off on his voyage home. But now that Mr Leyel wished to get a return cargo as soon as possible it would be wise to sail up along the coast. In Tranquebar there were few goods to be had.

Leyel turned the matter over, but he felt that if Pessart sailed off on his own there would be nothing to prevent his making off with all the ships and their cargoes, while he himself was completely ignorant of the present state of the Company. He did not trust the man, and was afraid of being made to look like a complete fool. So he agreed to their sailing northwards together as soon as Pessart had arranged his affairs, which, he said, would only take a couple of days.

Part of the *Christianshavn*'s cargo was unloaded, among other things a number of casks of wine from the Canary Islands. In the meantime Leyel wandered about the fortress trying to form an estimate of the amount of work to be done. He did not care for the way the fortress was run, especially when he realized how much alcohol was consumed. Almost no work was done. Pessart had promised that they would soon be leaving, but it was all of twelve days before he was ready. Leyel felt he could have arranged everything in a fraction of that time.

On Sunday, when Pessart and the majority of the men were gathered in the church, Leyel had King Christian's instructions read aloud, which stated that now Rytter had left, he and Pessart would alternate every month as the supreme governor of the Company's affairs.

But at last they left Tranquebar. Leyel had taken the precaution of stationing a couple of men he trusted on each of Pessart's ships and left others at Dansborg. But even now Pessart was in no hurry. He insisted that they visit the English station at Madras, where he had some accounts to settle with the English agent Francis Day, whose ship had lain at Tranquebar until August 9. Here they stayed for four days while Pessart caroused with his English friends. Leyel grew impatient. At last he had had enough. He left the boisterous company, went on board the *Christianshavn* and gave orders to sail immediately. A gun was fired to tell those on shore that they were about to weigh anchor, and when Pessart heard it he figured out that he had better leave. But he was furious and swore that Mr Leyel should live to regret it.

On September 25 the ships lay off Masulipatnam, where Leyel was pained to hear that the credit of the Danish Company in the town was completely ruined, that Claus Rytter had been put in prison twice because of Pessart's enormous debts, and had had to pay out a large sum of money to regain his liberty, that Pessart had also been to prison, and that his wife and children were still being held as hostages by his creditors – though some of the children were set free for a few hours so they could visit their father on board.

Consequently neither Pessart nor Leyel dared go ashore. Nor did the local inhabitants have any wish to trade with the debt-ridden Danes. Among the rumours on board was a tale of one of the Company's biggest creditors, a Muslim Mahmed Cossein, who had just gone to Jidda on the Red Sea hoping from there to travel overland to Copenhagen to demand his just claims. Another man, an Armenian, was said to have similar plans. A desperate measure for merchants threatened by ruin.

As Leyel realized that there could be no trade in Masulipatnam the ships continued north to Emeldy. Pessart paid several visits along the coast to see his friends – he seems to have had many – and the reunion was always celebrated with a lot of drink. Leyel went along a couple of times; but grew angry when he realized that Pessart was trying to make him so drunk that he could sail off without Leyel noticing it. The monsoon was approaching, and the little Danish fleet reached Emeldy at last, where the ships could be overhauled during the months in which it was impossible to sail. The *Christianshavn* had leaks both in the bows and the stern, and Leyel wanted to have the *Valby* sheathed with an extra layer of planks as a protection against the dreaded ship worm.

On October 10 when Pessart tried to move *The Bengali Prize* nearer the shore so as to unload, he was careless and the ship ran aground on a reef and was badly damaged. He did not seem to care, put up a tent on the shore and continued drinking with his companions. His goods were brought on shore and he sold a good deal, apparently without caring much about any profit or to which account the money was paid.

Several of the men came secretly one evening to Leyel and told him that they had heard Pessart boast when drunk that he planned to take the *Valby* and sail off with his men. He was not going to be called to account by such a fellow as Leyel. He was his own master, and he was going to prove it.

The news was only what Leyel had expected. On October 28, as soon as it was dark, he sent Jørgen Hansen with eight unarmed men over to the *Valby*, where they went on board and cut the cable – it would have made too much noise to heave the anchor in the usual manner, and they feared that Pessart and his men would attack them if they suspected what was happening. Shortly afterwards the sloop lay safely guarded under the *Christianshavn*'s guns. It had been a bit risky, for if Pessart had come out with his twenty armed men, there might have been a fight, and Leyel wished to avoid this.

Leyel immediately summoned the ship's council and then opened the letter with the secret instructions the King had given him with orders not to open it until it became evident that Berent Pessart had proved unequal to the trust placed in him. As might be expected the instructions were that if this proved to be the case it was the will of the King and the Company that Leyel take over the governorship, and that he should be recognized as the lawfully appointed governor by all the Company's employees. Since Pessart's plans to seize the *Valby* and sail off with it had been attested by witnesses it was decided to arrest him at once.

With a party of armed sailors Leyel rowed ashore and advanced on Pessart's tents. But here they discovered that Pessart had already fled with his fellow conspirators, and had only left some drunken men sleeping on their mats. It soon became apparent that a number of honest men had fled inland where they had hidden; but now that they saw what was happening they came forward and Leyel found out that Pessart had fled southwards with the barge a whole hour before they had come to arrest him. There were sixteen men with him, among others the mate from the *Christianshavn*, Peter de Sivart, whom Leyel had posted on Pessart's ship to keep an eye on him. Among the others was Pessart's captain, Michel Evertsen. They had apparently noticed that the *Valby* had been moved, and had then decided to make off with the barge which they had hastily loaded with some of the chests Pessart had in his tent.

From the men Pessart had left on the beach Leyel now discovered that not only had Pessart had plans of seizing the *Valby* but had had plans of setting fire to the *Christianshavn* in revenge for the humiliations he had suffered, and that he had already hired Indian catamarans for that purpose. Leyel immediately sent off Jørgen Hansen with the longboat and a strongly armed crew to try to overtake the barge. They did overtake them in the course of the night, and Jørgen Hansen shouted to Pessart that he must return and declared on behalf of His Royal Majesty that he was arrested. But Pessart was not going to surrender and shouted back that he would rather die. The longboat had a small cannon, and Jørgen Hansen now gave orders to fire on the barge. But Pessart had piled his chests up along the gunwales, and the heavy sea made it impossible to aim properly.

Jørgen Hansen pursued the barge all the way to the Petapuli Reef; but as Pessart had about a score of armed men who seemed determined to defend themselves Jørgen Hansen finally gave up and reported back to Leyel four days after he had left, while Pessart continued south towards Dansborg. Besides Peter de Sivart he also had with him the barber Joakim Caulitz, the gunner Marten Jansen, a couple of boatswains, the boy David Waltersen, and ten of his cronies. Leyel did not consider these men any great loss to the Company, but called them "drunkards and useless folk", people who felt more at home with Pessart's unstinted use of spirits and lack of discipline.

Mourids Christensen, who spent some time at Tranquebar a quarter of a century later, writes of the weather in November that there were continuous gales and storms: "now begins the great rainy season, the days draw in and grow dark, the nights lengthen and are inky black, both day and night there are continuing rain, thunder, and lightning. No ships or vessels are to be seen at sea, even the fishermen dare not set forth. There is a great commotion in the sea, wave rises against wave, the surf so violent that no-one can sail from the coast, no boat or the smallest vessel."

As long as this monsoon lasted there was no possibility of sailing in pursuit of Pessart. Besides, as already mentioned, the *Christianshavn* was leaking badly, and both ships were presumably partly stripped down, so all that Leyel could do for the time being was to send a messenger to Dansborg. The letter is dated November 18, 1643, and was addressed to the chief merchant Jacob van Stackenborg and "every officer and every man in our most gracious King's fortress Dansborg at Tranquebar". In his letter Leyel tells briefly of Pessart's flight and of how "because of his drunkenness and objectionable lifestyle" he had completely ruined the good name of Denmark in this country and he therefore commands that should Pessart arrive at the fort "they should without loss of time do their utmost to apprehend him" and take from him anything he has with him, both money, silver and gold, besides any other goods, as Leyel has been informed that it is a large amount, which must be presumed to belong to the Company and not to Pessart himself. Van Stackenborg and the other officials at Dansborg should at once enter the amount and guard the valuables carefully until Leyel comes himself, which he hopes will be in January.

He continues: "None of you should show the above-mentioned Berndt Pessart any obedience or submission, but esteem him a false and faithless fellow." They should see to it that he did not conspire with the Portuguese, to whom it was conceivable that he might try to sell the fortress. In return Leyel promised to pass over any fault or negligence they might be guilty of if only they would now obey his orders. He realizes that it is Pessart who is to blame.

At Emeldy work continued on the repairs to the ships. The *Christianshavn* was leaking both at the bows and the stern and was reinforced with fresh planks below the water-line; but they dared not draw her ashore because the keel was weak. The *Valby* was also sheathed with a double layer of planks.

Leyel ends his letter by noting that the *Valby* will soon be ready to sail, and that in four or five days he intends to send it to Bantam and Macassar to inform the Company's agents there, Herman Clausen and Nicolaj Samson, of what had happened and tell them to beware of Pessart if he should turn up. With regard to Pessart's wife and children still held in a debtor's prison at Masulipatnam the news is that Pessart had managed to send them a substantial sum of money before he disappeared. The money seems to have been stolen from Leyel on the *Christianshavn* by Pessart's servant Manuel, and Leyel believes it possible to extract the truth from Manuel "to which end I shall make use of extreme means if necessary". Torture was not unusual in those days.

He must have managed to get a message to the Islands in some other way for as soon as the *Valby* was ready to sail Leyel sent it off to resume the privateering war against the Bengalis. Almost at once, on December 14, 1643, the *Valby* had the good fortune to seize a large new ship off Narsepur. It was armed with the usual Indian guns, but faced with European cannon their guns were of little use. The ship was brought in to Emeldy, where the ship's council duly declared it a legal prize and paid prize money to the Danish seamen according to Christian IV's articles.

A new expedition in January 1644 brought a new prize with a load of Bengali linen, pepper, a little ambergris and some Chinese silk. The captain Abdul Gany and six Moorish merchants were taken prisoner. They seem to have been slave traders, for there were thirty-four slaves on board, mostly children, all carefully registered by the Danes:

1 slave girl, 12-13 years, now called Maria,
1 slave, 9-10 years, now called Matthæus,
1 slave, 7-8 years, now called Juan,
1 slave, 6-7 years, now called Bartholomæus,
1 slave woman, 22-23 years, now called Catharine,
1 small slave, son of Catharine, 3 years old, now Jørgen,
1 slave girl, 17-18 years, etc.

The slaves seem to have been baptized, were given good Christian names and were then presumably sold. It has been said that the Danes usually baptized and sold the whole crew on any vessel they seized; but is this correct? The name Abdul indicates that the captain was a Muslim, and Muslims are not usually willing to be baptized. Of course, one can get people to do most things by threatening to kill them; but is it not more likely that such men were held to ransom? It could not benefit trade relations to give more offence than necessary.

At about the same time Leyel learned that the *Christianshavn* had seized four Bengali vessels, one of them a large three-master on its way home from Achin (now Aceh) on the northern tip of Sumatra. On board there were, among various other things, five elephants ordered by the king of Golconda. Leyel at once had the elephants forwarded to the king as a gift from the Company. He then appointed his assistant on the *Christianshavn*, Hans Knudsen, as captain of this fine ship which they had decided to incorporate in the little Danish fleet and named it *The Little Elephant*. It was taken to Corengy where Knudsen was to have it repaired and armed with cannon.

In the meantime Pessart had arrived safely at the English station at San Thomé, but had to remain here for a fortnight because of bad weather. He then continued to Dansborg. In some way he had managed to intercept Leyel's letter and kept the messenger in confinement for the next few months.

Leyel may not have known what had become of Pessart. Apparently he was in no hurry to reach Dansborg, though he received no reply to his letter. He eagerly took part in the privateering ventures by which means he obtained some badly needed capital so that he could at least partly satisfy some of the Company's creditors.

It was early April before the *Christianshavn* anchored off the new English Fort St George (Madras) where Leyel seems to have been given a warm reception by the English agent Francis Day. There exists a letter from Day to "my highly esteemed friend William Leyel" stating that he had sent on board his ship all the fruit and vegetables his garden could produce.

On the evening of June 11, 1644, Whit Tuesday, the *Christianshavn* and the *Valby* again cast anchor in the road off the Danish fortress. But Dansborg showed no signs of life. No guns fired a greeting, no boats came out to welcome them, no official appeared on the beach. Unsure of what this might mean Leyel sent a letter with one of the fishermen to Dansborg, addressed to Jacob van Stackenborg asking him to send fresh provisions for the 140 persons on board as they had been at sea for some time. At the same time Leyel asked that some "white" official, i.e. a European, come to tell him how matters stood within the fortress.

But there was still no reply. Dansborg was as silent and inhospitable as before. So the following morning Leyel sent another letter, this time addressed to the chaplain Niels Andersen Udbyneder asking him to act as the "sensible and learned man" he was. Leyel describes his astonishment at receiving no reply to his letter the evening before and mentions his suspicion that this must be due to "the runaway windbag Pessart", who must have given orders to close the fort to Leyel and his men. If they now intended to adhere to these instructions "you may be sure that I will use even the most extreme measures, as is meet and proper, and to perform which I shall not lack the means … to punish rebels and perjurers, as both the Dutch and the English have promised me every assistance; still, I hope that it will not prove necessary to resort to such extreme measures."

Leyel goes on to refer to the royal instructions he had had read in the chapel at Dansborg the previous September providing for the alternate leadership of himself and Pessart. But added to this he can now refer to His Royal Majesty's most gracious instructions, which had been sealed and not to be opened until Pessart had proved himself unfit for his position. Leyel had opened these last instructions in the presence of the ship's council after Pessart had sailed off from Emeldy. On his way to Dansborg Leyel had shown these instructions both to the Dutch governor at Palicat and the English agent at Madras, and they had both promised to arrest Pessart as a traitor if they saw him, for according to the King's instructions he had now been removed from his post and thus had no right whatsoever to make a trading voyage on behalf of the Company to Japan or any other destination. He had also sent a message to Malacca as there was a rumour that Pessart intended to go there as well as to Bantam and Macassar.

The authorities at Dansborg ought now to see the King's instructions so that they might realize that Pessart no longer has any power to act, and for this purpose two or three representatives from the fortress should come on board to see them for themselves. Leyel assures them on his honour that the delegates will not be harmed. He quite understands that they had little choice in the matter.

But if neither the chaplain nor anyone else came out to the ship Leyel would have to resort to serious measures. He was in a hurry because he had a lot of goods he wished to unload before setting out on a new voyage. The letter is dated "the roads off Dannisborrig, June 12, 1644".

Leyel was furious at this insubordination. As if he had not had enough trouble with the Spaniards! Was he to have fresh problems with his own countrymen? As if there were not enough problems with the hopeless mess Pessart had left things in! Here he was with his ships, His Majesty's legally appointed commandant, and could not even enter the fortress! The Danes would be made a subject of ridicule up and down the coast. Would he have to take the fortress by force of arms?

That afternoon he finally received a letter from Dansborg signed by van Stackenborg, Niels Andersen Udbyneder, and several others. They write that they are ignorant of any royal decree as to the removal of Pessart as governor. They deny that they are rebels and perjurers, they consider themselves good and honest men who – God forbid – have never intended to disgrace the Danish nation. They only know Berent Pessart as an honest man and their rightful commander and hope that Leyel will not resort to using extreme measures. They consider themselves entirely innocent in this tense situation, and if it so happens that Leyel and Pessart have any quarrel, they can only hope that this will soon be settled. Niels Andersen states as his excuse for not coming on board the *Christianshavn* that he has a sore foot (one cannot help asking if his addiction to drink had brought on an attack of gout). The letter refuses to send out any refreshments for the men on board, and apparently they had sent a crier about the town to give notice that nobody was to bring water or provisions out to the ships or to venture on board.

Leyel remained off Tranquebar for four days in an effort to bring the garrison to their senses, but to no avail. They remained adamant. It was a case of open mutiny.

However, his two ships had been at sea for a long time, and they were in need of water and fresh provisions, so he weighed anchor and sailed on southwards to Carical. From here he sent a highly respected Portuguese,

Antonio Pacheco, to Dansborg with a copy of the royal orders and still another summons to van Stackenborg and the other officials to obey the King's instructions and open negotiations with Leyel so they could settle their differences.

This might have succeeded if it had not been for Niels Andersen. He apparently hated Leyel, jeered at his messenger and swore to revenge himself on all the cowardly wretches who dared to give in. He cursed the Portuguese delegate and threw him out of the fort. Even worse happened a few days later. Leyel had again anchored in the roads ready to besiege Dansborg if he had to, and Pacheco tried to sail out to his ship to report to him. Andersen, who happened to be near him in a catamaran with two European soldiers, gave them orders to shoot Pacheco. They fired three or four shots, but may have been wise enough to miss intentionally. Pacheco, who had his wife and children with him in his boat, certainly felt that his life was threatened, but managed to get safely on board the *Christianshavn*.

As Dansborg was still sealed off, Leyel went ashore on June 22 with seventy armed men, both "whites" and "blacks", and two small guns. He was received with great joy by the inhabitants of the town and the local merchants, who had suffered under Pessart's inefficient regime and the poor discipline he maintained among the soldiers. Now the inhabitants came with food and drink to the besiegers. The local adrigar at once offered to assist Leyel with his men. Leyel's little army camped behind a stone powder magazine about two musket shots from Dansborg's ramparts, and they blockaded the approaches, so that no more provisions could get through.

Leyel then sent yet another summons to "Jakob Stackenborg and all persons with him" that they "at once obey the instructions and orders given to you and to us all by our Most Gracious Sovereign which we should humbly submit to and obey". He also invites them to come out and inspect the King's letter and his credentials so that they can see for themselves that he is speaking the truth, and he again assures them that such delegates need not "in any way fear that we shall do them any harm".

The siege lasted for some time, for there came no reply from Dansborg. But the Indians, who apparently knew Leyel from former visits, welcomed him with open arms, fed his siege troops and looked forward to getting rid of Pessart and his governorship.

Finally the commander of the guard, Frantz Erkmand, and some of the more level-headed men from Dansborg came out. They admitted that

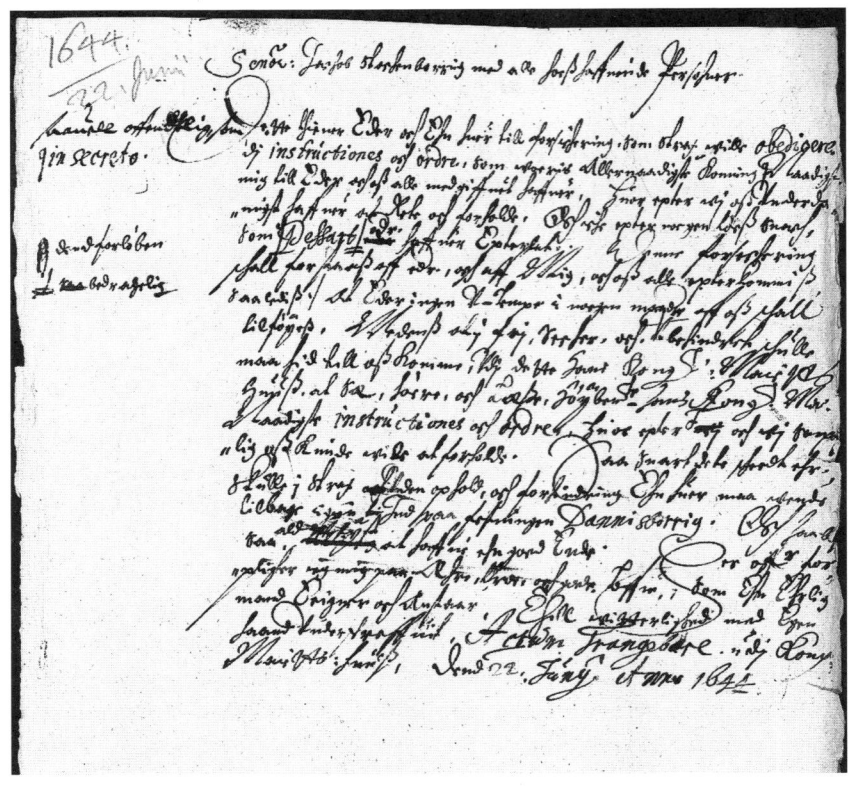

Leyel's letter to Stackenborg on June 22, 1644, appears to have been written in great haste and agitation. (Leyel's papers, The Danish State Archives.) The translation reads as follows:

Señor Jachob Stachenborrig and all persons with him.

This is to reassure all and every one of you who will immediately obey the instructions and commands that our most gracious king secretly has given me for you and us all which we should humbly obey. And not listen to empty words such as those the runaway Pessart has used to deceive you. This assurance must be taken to heart by you and me, and we must all obey it so that no injury may in any way be done to you by us. But so that you may come without hindrance and in safety to us in this His Royal Majesty's house to see, hear and read His Royal Majesty's gracious instructions and commands which you and all of us should obey. As soon as this is done, every one of you can immediately without hindrance return into the fortress. Thus I trust all will hopefully come to a good conclusion. Hereto I pledge my honour and faith as becomes an honest man.

Signed by my own hand. Given in Tranquebar in his Royal Majesty's house, June 22, 1644.

there was now a shortage of almost everything in Dansborg, deplored the manner in which Pessart had governed, and regretted the behaviour of the two clergymen, whose drunkenness and scandalous conduct had given offence to many. They reported that Pessart had openly boasted of how he had got hold of the letter Leyel had sent with the order to arrest him and had instead imprisoned the messenger. He had also sent out spies who had recently brought him the news that the *Christianshavn* was on its way, and only four days before Leyel's arrival Pessart had sailed off leaving written orders that the garrison must by no means recognize Leyel as governor. He was reported to have bought a Portuguese sloop, which he had named *The Good Hope*, and intended to make for Japan with a load of ray-skins, 30,000 according to some sources; but according to the Dutch Dagh Register perhaps more likely only 25 dozen, i.e. about 300. The skins were said to be easily available in the district around Tranquebar, but highly valued in Japan. Poor old van Stackenborg was now seriously ill and did not interfere in the running of the fort, so it was Niels Andersen who had led the opposition to Leyel.

Leyel now showed Erkmand and the other delegates the King's orders, upon which Erkmand promised on behalf of the garrison that they would surrender and recognize Leyel as their governor, if he on his side would promise to pardon them on behalf of the King. Leyel willingly accepted this. Mutiny was usually punishable by death, but here there were extenuating circumstances, and, besides, there were so few Danes in the country that one could not afford to be too strict.

The gates were opened, and Leyel and his men could at last take possession of the fort. It was in every way a sorry sight. There was not much left but the naked walls. In a letter to Hans Knudsen, hopefully busy with repairs to *The Little Elephant* at Emeldy, Leyel wrote how upon his arrival he had found "everything here in a bad way", and that Pessart with his drunken crew had "four days before our arrival absconded with a Portuguese sloop which he, Pessart, had bought in Negapatnam, and that he had taken all movables from the fort, and if they had been able to take the fort with them, they would not have left it behind". Besides which, he continued, "like most swindlers and men declared bankrupt" he had left his wife and children to their fate.

A closer inspection of Dansborg's buildings and fortifications was even more depressing than Leyel had expected. There did not seem to be a whole door or window frame in any of the houses; the white ants had hollowed out the woodwork so that it crumbled at a touch. And, as he had seen on his first visit, the walls had fallen into disrepair and the moats were half filled, partly with the fallen bricks, partly with every kind of rubbish which was apparently dumped here. It was not safe to cross the bridge across the moat, and the gate was liable to tumble down at any moment. Pessart had taken all the serviceable guns with him when he left, together with shot and powder, and most of the hand weapons. There were now only ten small iron guns for 3-4 pound shot, and even these were so badly damaged that they could be of little use.

It was rumoured that Pessart had taken 20,000 pieces-of-eight with him so that the Company's coffers were empty, apart from what Leyel had on board. And the warehouses were swept bare. Pessart seems even to have taken the Company's ledgers with him and left only debts and ill-will behind him.

The whole status of the Company was so bad that a lesser man might have given up, packed up in the course of a few days, and left for home. But Leyel was made of sterner stuff. Since the King had sent him out to order the Company's affairs he would do his best. He refused to give his former employers, the Dutch, any cause to gloat over the final defeat of the Danes in East India. If he persevered it ought to be possible to succeed.

Leyel had the greatest difficulty in forming a picture of Pessart's trade. Whereas the Danes had formerly maintained offices at Balasore, Pipeley, and Masulipatnam on the Indian coast, at Bantam and Japara on Java, and at Succadana and Mattam on Borneo, now it appeared that only Bantam and Macassar were left. And Pessart had ruined the trade on the Coromandel Coast to such a degree that it would be difficult to buy the usual cotton goods that could be sold at such a profit on the Islands – the trade that had been the basis of the Company's entire economy.

Nor did the garrison look any more promising. The men were lazy and much addicted to drink as there had been no proper discipline for a long time. Even the two clergymen were impossible, had caroused with the soldiers and disgusted the citizens by their conduct in the town. Claus Rytter had seen to it that Christen Storm was put in prison, where he had now been confined for three years. Leyel tried speaking with him, and as he promised to turn over a new leaf he was removed to the *Fortuna* on condition that he was not to go ashore.

On June 28 Leyel summoned the council and read out the sealed orders he had had from Christian IV. These had already been approved by the ship's council on board the *Christianshavn*; but now it was officially confirmed that Pessart had to be relieved of his command both because of his unfortunate management of the Company's affairs, and because he had now absconded and made away with as many of the Company's assets as he could lay his hands on. The meeting ended with the council noting that Pessart was said to owe 90,000 or 100,000 rigsdaler to Persian or Moorish merchants in Masulipatnam, so that no Dane would be able to obtain credit there.

They admitted that Pessart had been pursued by bad luck and many misfortunes he could not have foreseen, such as a voyage to Persia from which a whole load of goods were returned as they could not be sold, and the wreck of the *St Jakob*. On the other hand, the council found that it was imprudent to open a trade with new markets without first making sure that one could be sure of making a profit. The council's deliberations ended with the decision to relieve Pessart of his command, arrest him wherever he could be found, and to discontinue his monthly salary until he accounted for the goods and money in his keeping. This resolution is signed by Willem Leyel, Jørgen Hansen, the chief mate on the *Christianshavn* Carsten Ludvigsen, the second mate Simon Jansen van Medenblick, who had joined the ship in Spain, and boatswain Amund Olufsen who apparently had not learned to write and simply made his mark and set his seal under the other names.

Leyel now asked van Stackenborg before all the council what he could tell of the Company's finances. Had Pessart left any statement as to what capital or what goods the Company owned? Van Stackenborg could only say, No, there was nothing of that sort. Pessart had not even left money to pay their wages, but he had said that the garrison would have to manage on what customs they could collect in Tranquebar until he returned from Japan. Van Stackenborg also knew that they owed a large sum of money to the nayak, as the annual tribute had not been paid for a number of years.

Most of the accounts were in a mess, though it appeared that a monthly allowance was made to the wives of some of the men who had sailed with Pessart. The only other list was that of the Indians employed at Dansborg: the baker, the bricklayer, a dhobi (washerman), etc. One entry mentions a monthly sum to be paid to "Cutis Moeder, a woman whose husband had saved General Crappe's life when he lost his ship, the 'Øresund' off Carical". It was evident that van Stackenborg would not be of much assistance, and a few days later the old man died.

The council meeting ended by recognizing Leyel as the new governor, in agreement with what the King and the Company at home had decided, should Pessart prove himself unfit for the position.

For the time being, Leyel had no lack of things to put right. The excellent Indian bricklayers and carpenters were set to work rebuilding the walls and repairing the woodwork – Leyel had been so far-sighted as to bring some suitable wood with him from Narsapur. The ramshackle bridge was removed and a new stone bridge erected in its place. Leyel wrote home proudly that "This bridge will stand as long as the fortress exists". Little by little many of the houses were torn down and rebuilt, the gate and its archway were renewed, the church was repaired, and the entrenchments provided with counterscarps and palisades. A few guns from the *Christianshavn* were brought ashore and placed on the walls so that Dansborg would once more be able to defend itself. Leyel had also wanted to clean out the moat, but now the rainy season set in and it became evident that nothing more could be done before that was over, sometime in the new year.

Leyel also had some private matters to attend to. He had been informed that his stepdaughter Christina's husband had died in Java. Isaac Strycker had been dispenser to the fortress of Batavia, and, as Christina now was a widow and Isaac was said to have been quite well-to-do, he wrote asking the Danish agent there to find out whether Isaac had any surviving children or whether his stepdaughter was the legitimate heir. Leyel also expected Christina to come to Tranquebar in 1646, but apparently she never came.

On September 4 Leyel appointed a new man as acting governor when he could not be present himself. This was the reliable Anders Nielsen, who had already been in India for eight years, the man Claus Rytter had appointed as merchant on *The Gilded Sun*, and under his management Company affairs were again restored to order. The accounts can be seen to have been carefully kept from June 22. Frantz Erkmand was appointed to serve on the council. An able seaman from the *Christianshavn*, a man called Eskild Andersen Kongsbakke, whom Leyel had come to trust on the voyage, was appointed quartermaster at Dansborg, and by means of his quiet, but determined manner he quickly restored order to the garrison. Sentries were again posted on each of the fort's bastions and in front of the gate. A guard was appointed to make the rounds several times every night to make sure the sentries were vigilant. The soldiers were again made to drill and were schooled in the use of arms, so that little by little Dansborg was run as efficiently as ever. What nobody could know at the time was that many years later Eskild Andersen would become governor of Tranquebar.

CHAPTER 8

THE CLERGYMEN

Leyel had another problem. The two clergymen had caused a lot of trouble. Yet more proof that many men who at home in Denmark were capable of living respectable lives quickly degenerated in the tropics. The heat, the loneliness, the monotonous life in the fortress, and the lack of contact with friends and family at home could quickly undermine one's character. Everyone who had spent some years in the tropics knew several instances of good and honest men who simply went to pieces in the tropics; the heat seemed to drain all their moral stamina so that they sank into drunkenness and indifference towards the conventional moral standards they had held to before.

This had happened to the two clergymen. Niels Andersen Udbyneder had had a good character when as a young man he had been appointed chaplain on the *St Anna* on November 7, 1634; he was called "a zealous servant of the church". And when he had been appointed chaplain at Dansborg he had made the effort to learn Portuguese and preached in this language to the many Portuguese who had moved to the town. A number of the Portuguese Catholics who had been driven out of Porto Novo joined the Lutheran congregation at Tranquebar because of his efforts. At first he was always spoken of as an honest and learned man.

The other clergyman, Christen Pedersen Storm, was a Norwegian, from the town of Stavanger. He seems from the beginning to have taken the lead in their drinking and dissipation, but it gradually became difficult to say who of them was worse.

Claus Rytter had also received many complaints about the two clergymen, but had not quite known what to do about them. On January 25, 1642, he writes to Herman Clausen, who at that time was the chief agent at Tranquebar, about "our chaplain, Rev. Niels' shameful way of living, a disgrace to all Christian folk, and as long as that man continues at Tranquebar it will be our ruin among all the people. I desire that complaints of his evil deeds be brought before me by those he has injured, both among the Christians and the natives, together with written depositions so that we may have a firm ground on which to proceed, both at home and here. I should like to seize him, but do not know how this can be done without any disturbance. Please consider it, you know what I mean, but do not reveal anything, feign ignorance".

The fact was that both clergymen drank excessively of the strong Indian arrack and loved to invite Dansborg's soldiers to share in their drinking bouts, which naturally led to the breaking down of all discipline. But it was not merely their drinking. Their entire conduct gave offence both to the inhabitants of Tranquebar and throughout the whole neighbourhood where they were much talked of. Thus they sometimes ran in broad daylight through the streets stark naked, or with just a tiny loincloth – the Rev. Niels usually with a big sword in his hand.

On Sundays there was usually a market in the town square where the farmers from the whole district came with their goods. Here one could buy pots of the clarified Indian butter called ghee, poultry and eggs, coconuts and other fruits, rice, spices and betel, clay pots, jewellery – a festive sight. It is not clear if it was because of outrage at this desecration of the Sabbath; but one day the drunken minister came running, threatening people with his sword, kicked the clay pots so they were shattered into bits while the owners fled for their lives, the hens cackled, people screamed and ran, even the local Indian constable was scared and dared not oppose the minister. The Rev. Niels pursued them, constantly threatening them with his sword, and the whole market dissolved into screams and disorder. Finally, there was nobody left but a patient old horse tethered to his owner's two-wheeled cart, and so Niels struck at it with his sword till the blood flowed, and in the end the poor creature fell down dead. But even this was not enough to curb his rage – he began to strike the clay pots that were still intact so the ghee flowed into the dust.

When he finally withdrew to the fort the Indians slowly returned and there were loud cries of dismay when they found their goods ruined. The Muslim who owned the horse had suffered a ruinous financial loss and was furious. With the aid of some friends he dragged the dead animal to the fortress gate where he demanded to be admitted so the commandant might make good his loss. He was accompanied by many others. The broken pots were gathered in a heap and many wept and cried for help. But it was of no use. The only reply was that Pessart was not in the fortress, and the merchant van Stackenborg refused to pay any damages. The sentries on guard at the gate considered it all a, perhaps rather coarse, joke and found the Rev. Niels an amusing fellow. After the Indians had left, Niels got someone to skin the horse. For a long time he kept the skin, which naturally gave rise to teasing and crude banter.

The two clergymen's relations with women also caused much anger and gave offence to the inhabitants. Niels was said to have beaten and maltreated two Indian women so that they died, and now he was co-habiting with a Portuguese slave, whose Portuguese master had often demanded that she either be returned to him, or Niels at least pay him her price. But Niels paid no heed to such demands. In February 1644, under pressure from Leyel, he contracted a legal marriage with her, but abused her so badly that he ruined her health.

Rev. Christen Storm also married a Portuguese slave girl in spite of her bad reputation. It was said that because of her loose living she had been publicly flogged, mounted on a donkey and hunted out of her town, after which she had sought refuge at Tranquebar. But Storm, too, abused his wife so that she lost both her health and the use of her limbs.

One of the more entertaining stories that circulated in the town told of how the commandant of the Dutch station at Palicat had heard rumours of the shameful conduct of the Danish ministers, became curious and sent a corporal to Tranquebar to see if things really were that bad. He met Niels one Saturday evening when it was quite evident that he had been drinking heavily. One of the Company's men warned Niels that it would soon be Sunday and he was to conduct the service next morning. However, this did not disturb Niels. He answered cheerfully that there was nothing to it, and he could quite easily rattle off a sermon for the soldiers. When the time came he managed to appear in church and with some difficulty mounted the pulpit, but stood there talking a lot of nonsense. The congregation looked at each other, but nobody knew what to do. Niels finally came to a stop and seemed to fall asleep up there. A soldier ventured to go up and touch him on the shoulder. At this the minister woke up, but thought he was still drinking with his cronies and called out: "Ho! Fill the cup and take it to Herr Stackenborg!"

The story was naturally so entertaining that it was greeted with great hilarity by the Dutch and borne on the wings of gossip up and down the coast, not adding much to the reputation of the Danes. Leyel was furious and when he received a lot of both written and oral complaints about the two ministers he decided to remove Niels from the fortress as well, and sent him out to the *Christianshavn*. The belongings of both clergymen were put under seal until the complaints against them had been dealt with.

Shortly afterwards it was disclosed that Christen Storm had tried to persuade the crew of the *Fortuna* to make off with the ship. Leyel then had him put in chains and brought on board the *Christianshavn* where he was accused before the court on January 4, 1645; the court consisted of three members of the council at Dansborg and a couple of superior officers. Here Storm was confronted by the witnesses who had submitted complaints against him – including all the witnesses who could throw light on his conduct.

The records of the inquiry are still to be found in the Public Records Office in Copenhagen. The first witness, Jørgen Lauridsen, related how, when Rev. Storm had been put on board the *Fortuna* in September 1644, and the two of them were alone on board as the only whites among a number of coloured people, Pastor Storm had said one day when they were having dinner together that if Jørgen Lauridsen was of a like mind with him this was a favourable moment to make off with the sloop which was known to have a lot of goods on board. Storm had twice tried to talk him round; but Lauridsen had refused both times. Storm had then threatened him to keep quiet about this and swore that if he betrayed him Storm would of course say he was lying. That night Storm made great play of drawing his dagger and keeping it close at hand as if he intended to murder him while he slept. Lauridsen did not get much sleep that night, and the next few days Storm spoke a lot with the coloured people on board in Portuguese, a language Lauridsen did not understand. He became afraid that they were hatching a conspiracy to murder him and make off with the ship.

Later, when the *Fortuna* had reached Corengy both Pastor Storm and Jørgen Lauridsen were on board the *St Michael*. One evening when Jørgen Lauridsen lay in his berth in the cabin Storm came in and was obviously drunk; he stormed and raged and suddenly blew out all the candles. Lauridsen asked why on earth he did that and said that Storm would do better to go to bed. Storm had immediately turned on him and cried: "Are you there, you rogue? The Devil take you – you are just the one I am looking for!" Storm then attacked him in the dark and tried to stick his knife in him; but Lauridsen had been able to parry the blow with his arm which received a deep wound right in to the bone. Hearing the noise a member of the crew came running and shouted "Murder!" This brought several more men and they succeeded in seizing Storm and tying his hands and feet. Next morning Storm was fairly sober and asked them all not to tell what he had done.

Another witness, Jens Jensen Jyde, said that Storm had once asked if he would help him to make off with the ship to Achin on Sumatra, an invitation which Jens naturally said he had refused. He had been present in the cabin when Storm had attacked Jørgen Lauridsen, and had heard Lauridsen try to ward off the blow and exclaim: "You have wounded me as no honest man would do!" Jens Jensen had then shouted for help, upon which Storm had attacked him and tried to strike him with his knife several times, but he had managed to parry the blows with a small sword. Several people had then come running and disarmed Storm.

A third witness, Hans Pedersen, had been on board the *St Michael* when the ship lay off Emeldy loading goods. Pastor Storm and he had been sitting in the cabin when a storm blew up, and the *Fortuna* drifted out to sea. Storm had then said that he wished he had been on board the sloop: "If only I were there I should make the others sail off on our own venture; then Hans Knudsen would not have any power, and I could speedily persuade Anders, the constable. What good does the commander do you? You can expect nothing good from him – you would be better off to go with us. And you, too, Anders Thorkildsen – what do you think? You could all become rich in the sloop."

The statements were read aloud to Pastor Storm; he denied everything as being untrue and swore that he had never planned to make off with the *Fortuna*. However, the court refused to believe him, and admonished him to confess whether there were others implicated in the plans to seize the *Fortuna* and added that if he would not speak of his own free will they would have to use other measures. Storm blanched and exclaimed: "For God's sake, not that!" He now confessed that while the *St Michael* lay in Corengy roads, Jens Jensen had come to him several times and asked if they should not make off with the *Fortuna*, for, as he said, he believed that several others would be willing to join in. Storm then sounded out Hans Pedersen; but he had at once rebuffed him, saying "God preserve us from doing any such thing!" so that Storm had thought no more about it.

He could also remember that Pessart's mate Michel Evertsen, who at the time was captain of *The Bengali Prize*, had asked him once when they were at Tranquebar if they should not seize one of the ships. Evertsen had said that he, Jens Jensen, and a couple of the other whites would sail for Italy and mentioned places such as Naples or Venice. He was a mate, had learned to navigate, and could easily find his way.

The court then called Jens Jensen in and confronted him with Storm's statement but he swore that Storm had never spoken with him about seizing the sloop. He did, however, remember that Michel Evertsen had spoken of seizing the *Prize* and sailing to Masulipatnam where Berent Pessart was at that time. To this Storm replied that Pessart was not in Masulipatnam at that time, but was in Dansborg where he had been so angry with Evertsen that he had fired him as mate and instead appointed Simon Thorstensen.

The court now demanded that Pastor Storm sign the book as a confirmation of the various statements. Knowing that his signature would mean a death sentence, he refused categorically, upon which it was decided to examine him under torture. This was done in the presence of Leyel, the council, and the assembled crew. When they left off, he broke down and now confessed that all the statements were true, that Michel Evertsen was the first that had invited him to run with the ship and Jens Jensen the second.

His signature can still be seen in the records: "Christianus Petri Sturmius Stavangriensis. Christi potentissimi sangvine salvamur." (We are saved by the blood of the mighty Christ.)

Now the court had his confession they could proceed to the sentence: "We, the undersigned, have because of his dangerous plans and traitorous intentions according to our most gracious King's articles sentenced the above mentioned Christen Pedersen Storm to death. He shall this very day be put into a sack weighted with stones and thrown overboard and be drowned in the ocean." All his wages, belongings, and money were to be confiscated and forfeited to the King. His three slaves, a little boy named Antonio and two small girls, Maria and Dominga, were to be freed and funds should be taken from Pastor Christen's funds to care for them and give them a Christian upbringing. The sentence was signed by Willem Leyel, Jørgen Hansen, Poul Nielsen, the constable Rasmus Pedersen and boatswain Amund Olufsen.

The sentence may seem cruel but the crime was very serious: to make off with one of the Company's ships was to attack its very lifeblood; apart from the large value a ship with its load represented it was evident that there could be no trade without ships. Hence it was necessary to make an example.

The record continues: "On January 30 Christen Pedersen Storm was executed at sea about 4 leagues north of Dansborg, about 1 league off the shore" (see p. 112).

Oddly enough, no further action seems to have been taken against Jens Jyde, although it is hard to imagine that he was entirely innocent.

Pastor Niels remained in his prison until the autumn. In the meantime Leyel had had the opportunity to gather complaints about him from the townspeople and had time to examine the more serious charges.

The sentence passed on Christian Storm with his signature given as a result of being tortured: "Christianus Petri Sturmius Stavangriensis. Christi potentissimi sangvine salvamur" (We are saved by the blood of the Mighty Christ). (Leyel's papers, The Danish State Archives.) The translation reads:

When Christen Storm's confession was read aloud to him he refused to sign. Wherefore the commander and ship's council decided to use torture. He was then immediately examined under torture in the presence of the commander, the council and the whole ship's company. He freely confessed after the torture had been stopped that everything had happened as had been stated in the evidence. He then went through his confession admitting word by word that this was what he had said, he also explained that the skipper Michell Ewoutssen had been the first man ashore at Trankebar who had incited him to such a course of action. And that Jens Jyde had been the second who had done the same at sea on this voyage while we were away from Dansborg. As further confirmation he has with his own hand signed. Actum ut supra; Christianus Petri Sturmius Stavangriensis. Christi Potentissimi Sangvine Salvamur. Manu propria (with his own hand).

On October 1, 1645, the clergyman was finally arraigned before the council, which consisted of Willem Leyel, Jørgen Hansen, Anders Nielsen, Poul Nielsen, Simon Jansen, and the bosun Amund Olufsen. The written complaints over his many misdeeds, submitted by the many Portuguese who had settled in Tranquebar, were read aloud to him. The Catholic Christian inhabitants here said they had suffered much injustice, tyranny, and dishonour because of Niels Andersen Udbyneder's constant drunkenness as he often ran more or less naked through the streets and showered cuts and blows on many people using his iron weapon to wound them all without any distinction, no matter what class they belonged to.

The first complaint was about a Portuguese woman Anna Salazar, because the minister had forced his way into her house where he had attempted to rape her maid Lucretia, and when Anna would not permit this, he beat her with so many blows and so hard that she nearly died and had to stay in bed for three months. Anna was now called before the court to give her testimony, but she said that it was the late Pastor Christen Storm who had tried to rape her maid. But it was true that Niels Andersen had once run into her house. All the servants had fled in terror; only Anna remained as she was an elderly lady who could not run, and a girl, Francisca, whom Niels Andersen had grabbed and beaten about the head and body with a stick, and when she at last fell to the ground he kicked her until she no longer screamed. Anna had then said to him that the girl was dead and that he had killed her. This brought him somewhat to his senses, he went away, and they were able to take care of the girl who had to keep to her bed for seven months. But later Niels Andersen met Francisca in another house where he again fell upon her, and this time she died.

Anna Salazar further said that Niels Andersen had forced his way into her house several times with noisy threats and a bar from a door in his hand because she would not sell him some timber she had at half price. He had frightened her so badly that she had at last fled from her house and dared not move home again until he had been put in prison.

Another witness testified that a young Portuguese woman, May Giomar, one day during the Christmas season had been to Mass in the Catholic church and on her way home she passed Niels Andersen standing in his doorway. May Giomar greeted him as she passed. Suddenly, without the slightest provocation, Niels Andersen had assaulted her with his wooden bar and had beaten her so violently that he had broken her right arm and right thigh. The witness had seen it happen, but dared not intervene. May Giomar had collapsed in the street and had lain there until her eighteen-year-old son had arrived and carried her home to the small house she owned on the respectable citizen Michael von Danzig's land where she had had to lie in bed. She was unable to speak and was thought to have lost her reason. She died about a year later.

Yet another Portuguese girl, Michel Cotino's wife, Philippa Texera, was mentioned. Niels Andersen had for no reason at all attacked her in the street, beaten her with his stick so she got a deep wound in her breast, and kicked her when she fell. She had been lying at death's door for ten days, and lost her unborn child at three or four months.

Another witness, the above-mentioned Antonio Pacheco, who was considered one of the most respected Portuguese in Tranquebar, told how Niels Andersen had harmed both his honour and his goods. One day he had been sitting peacefully talking with Herman Clausen Rugmand in the porch outside his door when one of his servants came home from the market. At that moment Niels Andersen suddenly rushed out of his house with the familiar bar in his hand and beat the man so violently, and quite without provocation, that he lay as dead on the ground. He had had to lie in bed for three months and then moved to another town for fear of the minister.

Another day one of Pacheco's servant girls came carrying a large pot of water from Anna Salazar's house. He struck her with the bar so that she lay unable to speak for twelve hours and had to keep to her bed for two months. Pacheco also told how his wife had once been home alone behind locked doors; the minister had come and thundered at the door, and when she did not open he had abused her with the grossest insults. Pacheco also mentioned the time when Niels Andersen had given the soldiers orders to shoot at him when he was on his way in a boat to tell Leyel whether he had been successful in his attempts to persuade the minister to surrender the fortress.

Juan Borges, another highly respected Portuguese, whom Leyel had recently sent as interpreter with a delegation to the king of Candy, could also tell of an injury, though of a less serious nature. Niels Andersen had taken a fancy to his parrot, and one day he had forced his way into the house, together with two soldiers from the fortress, and made off with the bird. During his examination Niels Andersen denied that this was true. He claimed that a soldier had presented him with the parrot as a gift. But nobody believed him, and Leyel immediately had the parrot fetched and delivered to its owner.

Yet another Portuguese, Manuel Machado, had suffered an injury as a Danish soldier Oluf Christensen testified from his own observation. One day he had seen the said Manuel Machado standing tied to an anchor by order of Berent Pessart; unfortunately the man stood just below Niels Andersen's window, where the minister stood, very drunk. Christensen had seen him take the bar from the window and throw it down on the defenceless Portuguese, who had received a large wound to his head. It had bled badly, as wounds to the head do, and the man had had to keep to his bed for two months before he regained his health.

A Portuguese merchant, Juan Alvarez, from Negapatnam, who often sailed to the town with his goods in his sampan, had once lodged a complaint with the court at Dansborg, where Jacob van Stackenborg then was the chief authority. The fact of the matter was that the woman with whom Niels Andersen was living without being married to her was a slave girl belonging to Alvarez's mother-in-law, for which reason he demanded that the minister at least should pay compensation for her loss. At this Niels Andersen became so furious that he struck Alvarez several times in the face before the court, and finally knocked him over and went on hitting and kicking him. Van Stackenborg had merely looked on, and none of the others present had the courage to interfere either; Niels Andersen was evidently a very big and strong man, and when he was angry nobody dared oppose him.

Poul Nielsen had witnessed the scene in the court and felt it was scandalous that the authorities at Dansborg let the drunken minister behave in this way. They could have called for help. Whether the authorities were afraid that the soldiers would side with Andersen is not clear, but it is more likely that it was the will to interfere that was lacking.

In any case Alvarez had been hurt so badly that he had to keep to his bed and was bled several times before he regained his health. After that he dared not come to town with his goods. A number of other merchants were now afraid to come to Tranquebar, which was naturally injurious to the town's trade and the income from the customs.

A Japanese soldier, Thomas Dono, who was serving at Dansborg, had stood guard one evening on the walls when he heard Niels Andersen in a violent quarrel with Pessart in the courtyard. When they began to fight Dono ran down to help the president; but the minister had then stuck a dagger in his breast. It bled profusely, but he had recovered. He could tell how the drunken minister had played havoc in the town, coming to blows both with van Stackenborg and the chief of the guards Erkmand,

and attacking everybody regardless, like a wild bull or an untamed tiger. The witness added that as a result of the minister's actions Tranquebar had got a bad name all over East India, and that because of Niels Andersen Udbyneder His Majesty's castle and all the Danes had become objects of contempt and ridicule.

The Muslims in the town also submitted a written complaint to the court written in Portuguese. They told how Niels Andersen one market day under the influence of alcohol had beaten a poor merchant's horse to death and also smashed four large clay pots with oil. He had also mal-treated one of the most distinguished men among them, a man called China Maraa, whom all the governors of Tranquebar had employed as interpreter before the nayak of Tanjore, and he had often helped the Danes in their negotiations with the nayak, invaluable assistance as he knew the local customs. Niels Andersen had also beaten him with his stick, driven him before him with blows and finally put him in irons and chained him to a large tree outside his door – an action that had caused great indignation in the town. There was still another man, Chenata Pule, whom the minister had beaten and had also taken pig's manure from the street and stuffed it into his mouth – a disgusting thing to do especially in view of the loathing with which Muslims regard the pig and consider it an unclean animal whose flesh they will never touch.

They also mentioned an Indian woman, Waidy, who often came to town to sell firewood. One day, when she was ready to leave for her vil-lage about half a mile away, she was passing Niels Andersen standing in his doorway with a big stone in his hand, when he rushed out and beat her about the face and head so that she was badly wounded and there was a lot of blood. She was helped home to her village, and here she lay for six months, had to have medical care in order to regain her health and finally had to sell her only son, a boy of about ten, in order to pay the bills. She appeared in court and showed that her face was badly scarred.

Finally, the Danish soldiers from Dansborg testified against Niels An-dersen that when he was drunk he beat whoever was near him, even van Stackenborg himself, called them dogs and scoundrels and struck out at them so nobody could feel sure of his life. On Easter Monday he had broken Jacob Amager's arm and furthermore put it out of joint, and he had broken one of Jens Madsen's ribs so that the poor man had been seriously ill for a long time.

The above-mentioned Jacob Amager and two other soldiers told how they twice had had to drag Niels Andersen out of a brothel in the town where he visited a certain Natalia; he was then quite drunk and stark naked. Another time, the Indian soldiers, the taliars, had dragged him by his feet along the street up to Dansborg, mother-naked, to the outrage of the whole town.

The highly respected citizen Michael von Danzig, who had come to Tranquebar with the first Danish ship and had lived there ever since, told how when Niels Andersen had been put in prison because of a violent attack on van Stackenborg, von Danzig's wife had borne a child that was not not going to live. He wanted it baptized and applied to Pastor Storm, who said that he could not baptize the child because he had been unfrocked. The father then applied to Niels Andersen, who refused to baptize it in the prison; but van Stackenborg feared for his life if he let him out, so finally von Danzig had baptized his own child as every Christian has the right to do.

It was also said that Niels Andersen had for a long time cohabited with the woman he now finally, because of Leyel's request, had agreed to marry; but he had beaten her so badly that she was both a cripple and could not stand straight. And Leyel considered it both as lèse majesté and mutiny that Andersen had refused him admittance to Dansborg and refused to obey the King's orders although Leyel had informed him of the King's instructions.

When all the witnesses had been heard Niels Andersen was asked if he would confess to these things. However, he refused categorically and said that it was all a pack of lies. The court then decided to torture him as Pastor Storm had been, but asked him once more if he would not sign voluntarily as everything had been examined so carefully and the accusations confirmed by so many witnesses. He then gave in and signed. However, he maintained that the said persons had not died from the blows he had given them; but, on the other hand, he admitted that he had not been reconciled with any of them before they died.

The court then proceeded to pronounce sentence: "Since from all the above charges and these testimonies thereunto as also according to the above mentioned Pastor Niels Andersen Udbyneder's own confession it is evident that the above mentioned Pastor Niels Andersen Udbyneder was the cause of the death of the said women May Giomar and Francisca, as also that the the woman Philipa Teixera whom the above mentioned Pastor Niels Andersen has beaten and maltreated as stated, so that he caused her to lose her unborn baby, and furthermore, that Pastor Niels Andersen Udbyneder during almost the whole period he has been in the fortress of Dansborg has lived in constant drunkenness, moral looseness and disorderly fights, and maintained a very un-Christian and ungodly way of life which has seemed scandalous and horrible to all men, as stated above.

"For this reason we the undersigned councillors have in accordance with our most Gracious King's articles and instructions sentenced the said Pastor Niels Andersen Udbyneder to death. And he is to be put into a sack weighted with stones and thrown into and drowned in the sea here off the road opposite the fortress Dansborg, as an example to all men that they keep themselves from such ill deeds. And all the wages due to the said Pastor Niels Andersen Udbyneder are to be confiscated and revert to our most Gracious King.

"All other goods and everything else, though of small value, he leaves behind him shall belong to his surviving wife Monica, and she shall have full power to enjoy and keep it so as to support and sustain herself therewith.

"Witnessed by us the undersigned with our own signatures. Given this day in the fortress of Dansborg on the Coast of Coromandel, October 3, Anno 1645." Signed W. Leyel, Jørgen Hansen, Poul Nielsen, Anders Nielsen, Simon Jansen, and chief bosun Amund Olufsen's seal and mark.

In spite of the many injuries the people of Tranquebar had suffered at the hands of Niels Andersen they felt that when he had been sober he had been a wholly different man, and especially at first he had been an industrious, learned, and good clergyman. They felt that it was Christen Storm who had made him a partner in his drunken orgies. And, curiously enough, a few days after the sentence had been pronounced, the council received a number of pleas from the Christians, both among the Europeans and the Indians, asking that he be pardoned, or at least that the death sentence not be carried out.

Consequently, the council commuted the death sentence to exile. The minutes state: "Since all our fellow Christians, both the Europeans and their wives, and, similarly, all the Indian Christians here with great earnestness asked and desired the Governor and us the undersigned that Pastor Niels Andersen Udbyneder be pardoned and his life preserved, we the undersigned have on behalf of his Royal Majesty revoked the death sentence. But on condition that the said Pastor Niels Andersen leave this country and never may the said Niels Andersen Udbyneder dare to come to the Coast of Coromandel, and still less here to the fortress of Dansborg or the town of Tranquebar. Should he be found on this Coast of Coromandel the authorities serving our most gracious King here at the fortress or at any other places on the said Coast of Coromandel shall at once arrest the said Pastor Niels Andersen Udbyneder and then immediately without mercy in accordance with the above sentence execute the said Niels Andersen Udbyneder in the manner stated above. Everything else that was resolved in the above mentioned sentence regarding the said Niels Andersen Udbyneder's monthly wages, goods, house, etc. shall be dealt with as stated in our previous sentence." This addition to the sentence is dated October 8.

Niels Andersen was then sailed to Ceylon and put ashore in a deserted place on the coast with some food and left to his fate. Somehow or other he succeeded in reaching the port of Cotiari which was occasionally visited by the Company's ships that came partly to trade, partly to have the ships repaired. Apparently he did not reform his style of life and spoke ill of the Danes whenever he could. His wife Monica was allowed to keep the house and furniture, but her husband's wages reverted to the King, so we do not know how she managed to live. Presumably the Company granted her a kind of widow's pension as was the case with other widows who had survived men employed by the Company.

CHAPTER 9
THE FATE OF BERENT PESSART

Berent Pessart had sailed from Tranquebar on June 5, 1644, just a few days before Leyel arrived. He had taken everything he could lay his hands on of the Company's goods, money, and equipment, and had high hopes of making a good bargain with his ray-skins which were said to fetch huge prices in Japan, where the Japanese made various luxury articles from the skins. The Dutch had discovered this market in Japan in 1635 and found that the skins could be sold there at a good profit. The Dutch had then tried to buy up all the ray-skins from San Thomé and all along the coast so as to gain a monopoly; but Pessart had somehow succeeded in procuring a sizeable quantity of the skins. They had been packed carefully in the hold of *The Good Hope*, the name he had given the little sloop he had bought off the Portuguese at Negapatnam. It may be that he dreamed of returning to Dansborg with such a large fortune that Leyel would not be able to hold his own. Or had he intended to sever every connection with the Company? At any rate he intended to turn his back on Leyel, whom he hated, and the humiliations he would have to face at Dansborg. But he was something of a dreamer, and his hopes were probably somewhat unrealistic.

Pessart had sailed east in order to pass through the Malacca Straits on his way to Japan. However, the Dutch had seized Malacca from the Portuguese in 1641, and the Dutch East India Company kept a sharp lookout for all the ships that passed through the Straits. They were afraid that other nations would interfere with their monopoly on the spice trade with the Islands.

When Pessart had entered the Straits the wind died and while they lay becalmed the crew spent their time drinking – there may have been a store of Leyel's good Canary sack on board. There happened to be a Dutch ship nearby, and the Dutchmen sent their mate over to ask what ship it was and inquire about their destination. The mate was invited to share their drink; but this turned out to be a doubtful pleasure, for the Danes were very drunk. A quarrel soon broke out, and the Dutch mate came to blows with Pessart's mate, Michel Evertsen. It turned into a real fight, from which the Dutchman only escaped with torn clothes and a number of wounds.

When the mate returned to his own ship and the officers saw how he had been treated they quickly agreed that such treatment was unacceptable, and as they thought there was something very suspicious about the ship – Pessart can hardly have dared tell them that they were on their way to Japan and may have stammered a bit when asked about his destination – the Dutchmen sent a boat over full of armed men who would have found the drunken Danes easy game. They did try to defend themselves, but could hardly stand upright. Pessart was wounded in the foot by a spear and put in prison with the rest of the crew. It is difficult to say how many were killed or wounded, but we are informed that the *Christianshavn*'s former mate Peter de Sivart and several others died on the way to Batavia, and it is quite likely it was here. The surviving Danes were imprisoned in the hold, a Dutch prize crew was put on board, and the ship taken to Malacca.

Here the Danes were kept in prison for three months, while *The Good Hope* was judged a lawful prize and confiscated with all its goods.

Pessart, who had once lived in Batavia and had a certain status protested so strongly against this treatment that the authorities finally agreed to bring the ship and its crew to Batavia and bring the whole matter before the court there. At Batavia the ship's goods, rudder, and sails were taken into custody, and another six months passed before Pessart was set free. Batavia was notorious for its unhealthy climate and during the long wait another ten of Pessart's original thirty-six men died. His persistent efforts finally resulted in his getting his ship back together with the pitiful remainder of the crew, but the ray-skins to which he had pinned such great hopes were confiscated and he was forbidden to sail to Japan.

The fact was that all trade with Japan was a delicate and dangerous affair. In 1640 the Portuguese had sent a delegation to Japan in an attempt to establish trade relations. However, Japan did not want any contact with the outside world and, to emphasize this, sixty-one members of the delegation were executed out of hand and their heads set on stakes as a warning to other Europeans who might have similar plans. A few men were left alive and sent back to tell their countrymen that they were unwelcome here.

The Dutch had had better luck. Just in 1641 a small island off Nagasaki had been assigned to them where they were permitted to establish what might be called an enclosed trading station, a place where they could exchange their goods for Japanese wares, but they were not allowed to move outside the island, and all trade was strictly regulated by the Japanese. The whole arrangement was new and relations with the Japanese so delicate that they had no desire to have other European nations ruin it all by interfering.

After six months in prison Pessart and his men had their sloop returned to them, and instead of the ray-skins he was supplied with a cargo consisting of pepper, cinnamon, linen, and other textiles; but apparently only on condition that he should bring this cargo to Manila in the Philippines and spy on the town's harbour and defences, as the Dutch were planning an attack on the Spaniards there in order to gain mastery of the islands.

Pessart complained that he had lost so many men, including his mate, that it would be difficult to undertake such a voyage. The governor, Anthony van Diemen, then gave him ten new men, nine of whom were Danes, presumably men who had come to Batavia on Dutch and English ships. But the tenth man, the new mate, was Dutch, which was presumably not merely by chance. It was later pointed out that Pessart had expressly desired a Danish mate, but the Dutch had replied that there were none. Later the men also maintained that they had had no idea as to their destination, and not until they were at sea had Pessart mustered the crew, made them swear allegiance to the Danish king and told them they were going to Manila.

Somehow Leyel heard of these plans, and as he was afraid that they might harm Danish trade, he felt obliged to inform the Spanish general, who that year had come from Manila to Macassar. If the Danes lost their right to trade at Macassar it would be a hard blow, and what else could they expect if it was proved that a Danish captain had spied in Manila for the Dutch.

When they reached the Philippines Pessart's Dutch mate had difficulties finding the Bay of Manila, and by mistake he entered another bay where they dropped anchor in the hope of finding someone to direct them. But the place seemed to be uninhabited, so they decided to stay for a few days and provide the ship with fresh water and firewood and repair their sails. They remained for a week; but on the seventh day Pessart rowed out with the boat and some people to fish in the bay. They caught three large fish, and the men settled on the beach while Pessart cleaned the fish and the cook lit a fire.

While they were thus employed some natives stole out of the woods with their bows and arrows, shot Pessart, the mate, and a Lap who had served Pessart for a long time. Pessart managed to stagger out to the boat, where he and his servant were dragged on board, while he gasped: "Help me up, or I am a dead man!" There was only one oar in the boat, so they had to row with the thwarts, but managed to get out to the ship. Pessart had said no more and was already dead when they hauled him on board. That night they buried him on a small island in the bay. A sad ending to all his glorious dreams.

Since the captain was dead and the mate wounded Michel Evertsen took command, and it was decided to continue to Manila since they had come this far. But it took them all of ten days to find the town. Here the Spaniards made them welcome, and Evertsen managed to sell their goods, very profitably it was said, as the goods that had been bought at Batavia and valued at 12,000 rigsdaler were sold at Manila for 40,000. While Evertsen managed the trade the Dutch mate rowed about the harbour and drew plans of the harbour and the fortifications. Nobody seemed to have the least suspicion. By November they had both finished their work, and the ship lay ready to sail a small distance from the town when a storm blew up. So Michel Evertsen decided to postpone their departure – a fatal decision – for that very night one of Pessart's slaves, a man called Isaac, broke out of the prison where he had been confined for some misdemeanour. He was eager for revenge for the treatment he had received, so when he succeeded in swimming ashore he went straight to the commandant of one of the Spanish fortresses and told him that the ship came from Batavia and there were Dutchmen on board, and that he had seen the Dutch mate sounding the depth all over the harbour and drawing sketches of the fortifications. All this was naturally immediately reported to the Spanish governor of Manila, who at once had *The Good Hope* stopped. The ship and all the goods were confiscated and examined. The Spaniards found the mate's sketches and notes, together with his instructions from the Dutch authorities at Batavia. There could be no doubt. According to Spanish law the crew were given a lawyer to defend them and were permitted to appeal to the King of Spain – not much help, as it might be several years before they could hope for an answer. In the meantime the crew were put in irons and sent to the galleys, while the skipper Michel Evertsen and the barber Joakim Caulitz were put in prison and sentenced to death as spies. Three of the sailors were examined under torture; but as they were entirely ignorant of the espionage, they could not tell anything.

When in the early summer of 1646 Leyel was at Macassar with the *Christianshavn* he found that a letter had arrived addressed to the head

123

of the trading station there. It was dated January 8, 1646, at Manila and signed by thirteen members of Pessart's old crew.

It reads: "But that night a lascar (an Indian sailor) swam ashore and said that we were Dutch and rascals and thieves and traitors and spies, all of which is a lie, we know no more of it all than the child born last night. Then the authorities made us prisoners and put us in separate houses so that we could not talk together and examined us. We have told the truth, they have tortured three of us, but they told the simple truth, and this we are ready to die for. They have taken the ship and the goods and have sentenced the master and mate to death twice. They have sent us poor folk, except for the master and the mate, to the galleys and have shaved our hair and beards off and made us slaves, saying we must wait for instructions from Spain or Denmark." It continues: "We are as miserable as one can be in this world, and get nothing to eat but a handful of rice. Our master Michel is so strictly imprisoned that he cannot write to you."

After he learned how badly things had gone for Pessart and his crew Leyel wrote a letter to the governor of the Philippines asserting the innocence of the captured Danes in the espionage of which they had been accused and demanding their release and that the ship and goods be returned, emphasizing that they belonged to the Danish king. He maintained that when Pessart had been seized by the Dutch in the Straits of Malacca he had not had any evil intent, but had simply chosen the shortest route from India to Japan. He deplored that the Danish seamen had been arrested and the King's goods confiscated merely on the testimony of an escaped slave.

A copy of the letter was sent to the Portuguese viceroy in Goa so that he could forward it to his king. Leyel also sent letters home to King Christian both by English and Dutch ships telling what had happened in the hope that something could be done through diplomatic channels.

Leyel also sent a letter to the Danish prisoners at Manila telling them that he had written to the governor asserting their innocence in any espionage and had requested that they be set at liberty, and he had likewise protested against the injury the seizure of the ship had done to Danish interests. He also informed them that already the previous year he had mentioned their voyage to Manila in letters he had sent King Christian with Dutch and English ships and he hoped that the King could do something towards restoring their freedom. As for himself he would continue to work for their release "in which cause I shall spare no efforts".

But Leyel was of course also interested in regaining some of the seized goods and asked the letter-writer to tell him how large a sum of money the Spaniards had confiscated. He also knew that Michel Evertsen had written a letter to his sister at Tranquebar from his prison, but the letter had been confiscated. He finishes by assuring them yet again that he will do his best for them, and also for Evertsen and Caulitz.

The sources do not reveal the ultimate fate of the poor seamen. But one must doubt that they were released. Their companionship with Pessart had cost them dear.

CHAPTER 10

"LAUS DEO IN TRANQUEBAR"

King Christian IV had tried to counteract the increasing Swedish influence in Germany, and as the Swedes had already been provoked by the king's repeated increases in the Sound Dues, they felt that they had to act. The very day that Hannibal Sehested celebrated his mariage to King Christian's daughter Christiane, November 6, 1643, the Swedes without any declaration of war marched across the borders of Holstein under the command of Lennart Torstensson. He quickly occupied the whole of Jutland, and at the same time the Swedes attacked Scania, a Danish province on the other side of the Sound. There were sea battles at Lister Dyb and Kolberger Heide. The Danes were outmatched and in the late summer of 1645 King Christian had to sign an ignominious peace.

The news of all this was slow in reaching India; but it gradually became evident to the Danes out there that in such times neither the King nor the Company had the means to send new ships to the East. So in Tranquebar there could be no prospect of any assistance from home. They would have to manage as best they could. And there were many problems. Pessart's regime had left Leyel in a very weak position. The plan had been to send the *Christianshavn* home immediately with a good cargo; but there was no cargo ready, and as things were at present it would not be safe. There was the danger of the ship being seized by the Swedes as long as there was open war between the two nations. Once peace was declared it might be possible to procure a reasonable cargo, but there was another great difficulty, for Leyel did not think he could spare enough men to take the vessel home.

Through all the years he spent in India the lack of men was a constant difficulty. If the Company really wanted a Danish base out here Dansborg had to be properly manned with a force of Danish soldiers. These could of course be supplemented with Indian men; but without a solid backbone of Danes the colony could hardly survive. The problem was the steady loss of competent men. The climate was unhealthy for Europeans. Many died, others ran away, and still others were so often drunk that they were not of much use. In a report from 1644 Leyel writes that there were only seventeen white men at Dansborg, and of these at least ten were men from other nations, Englishmen, Portuguese,

Dutchmen, and two of the Danes so far gone in drink that they were of little use.

Besides manning the fortress men were needed to work the ships. Here the same rules applied: one had to make do with the few Europeans available and supplement these with Asian sailors, the so-called lascars, who made a valuable contribution over the years. The papers keep repeating the names of the few reliable Danes, so that one gradually gets to feel that one knows them. On the *Christianshavn* the captain was still Jørgen Hansen Riber. For a time the mate was Nicolaj Samsing, who came from the island of Samsø, so that in Danish the epithet Samsing was added to his name, just as Jørgen Hansen, who must have come from the town of Ribe on the west coast of Jutland, is given the epithet Riber, and the name of the town Korsør is added to Poul Hansen's name. (At this period Danish names were so stereotyped – Poul, Hans's son, became Poul Hansen, etc. – that in the muster rolls the name of the hometown was often added to the name.) It was probably the English who gave Samson his new name – presumably he was so big and strong that it suited him. For some years he had captained the *St Jakob* until it was wrecked on the Bengali coast, and he was one of the few who escaped with his life and made his way back to Tranquebar. After that Pessart employed him as master of the *Fortuna* and later Leyel employed him in the same capacity on the *Valby*, and on one occasion sent him as a delegate to the king of Candy in Ceylon.

The chief boatswain on the *Christianshavn*, Amund Olufsen, is mentioned fairly often – apparently he could neither read nor write, as he always merely sets his seal under the documents he has to sign. The ship seems at this time to have had a crew of thirty-eight, the majority of whom must have been lascars or belonged to other nations.

Anders Nielsen, whom Claus Rytter had appointed merchant on *The Gilded Sun* on his voyage to Macassar in 1642 also became one of Leyel's mainstays; he was the man he appointed to deputize for him at Dansborg when he himself was away on his voyages, and Anders Nielsen proved a very good and reliable support, who showed himself equal to the situation when the nayak's army attacked the town and he was responsible for the defence. Later Leyel used him both as a delegate to the nayak at Tanjore and as merchant on a voyage to Macassar.

Poul Nielsen was another of Leyel's loyal supporters. He had come to India probably with the *St Jakob* or the *St Anna* and had for a time served as merchant at the station in Pipeley, from which he escaped after having been imprisoned by the Bengalis. Finally there were a couple of men Leyel used as captains on the two sloops, Simon Torstensson and Simon Jansen van Medenblick – the latter name seems to indicate that he was Dutch.

It was these six or seven men who seem to have been the only ones Leyel dared give any real responsibility, and he had to keep shifting them around to fill the various offices. It was evident that there were far too few men, and in his letters home to the Company he constantly asks for more and more reliable people. Until these arrived he had to manage as best he could: "we must row with the oars we have", he wrote.

Nor were there many ships. The *Christianshavn* and the two sloops, the *Fortuna* and the *Valby* constituted the whole fleet, though this could be supplemented by the *St Michael* which they had seized from the Bengalis, and there was always the possibility of buying local sampans.

During the five years in which Leyel was the governor of the Company in India no new ships or men arrived, and apparently not even any letters from home. But he himself was scrupulous in sending detailed reports home, and it is from these papers, now stored in The National Archives in Copenhagen, that we are able to follow his movements.

During these years the Dutch advanced all over the region; but, according to Leyel, their often brutal actions led to the result that "the Dutch now begin to be hated and have a bad reputation in all the trading posts in India, and everywhere they are more feared than loved, and the Indians prefer to trade with us and the English."

About Tranquebar he writes in November 1644 that many Portuguese are moving to the town, since they have been forced out of Porto Novo, Negapatnam, San Thomé, and from Ceylon where the Dutch had taken Trincomalee in 1639. Everywhere the Portuguese feel themselves crowded out by the Dutch who are seeking to increase their power in the East. In 1643 the Dutch had attacked Ceylon with a fleet of fourteen ships and 2500 soldiers, but with no success as they had lost half their men. In 1644 they had had to give up an attack on the old Portuguese base of Goa on the west coast of India. But they had better luck elsewhere.

Leyel promised the Portuguese refugees security of life and property under Danish law. Some of the refugees were employed as soldiers and minor officials, while others took part in the coastal trade. Many natives moved to the town where trade was flourishing. Leyel thought that in this manner the town would soon be as large as Elsinore. There was complete freedom of conscience. Leyel naturally let the Hindus keep their temples and the Muslims their mosques, but he also gave the Portuguese refugees permission to build a large Catholic church – he writes that it will be as large as Holmens Kirke in Copenhagen. He seems to have been more liberal than most of his men. There is a letter to him from Niels Andersen Udbyneder, Frantz Erkmand, and the highly respected citizen Michael von Danzig dated July 11, 1644, mentioning that the Catholics through their priest, Padre Agostino Lend, are asking for permission to buy the Rev. Christen Pedersen Storm's house in order to use it as their church. The writers beg Leyel to refuse this request as they are afraid that their children will be infected with the Catholic faith. They admit that perhaps they are afraid of acting like the goose who admitted the fox which then ate her and her young. But Leyel refused to succumb to this fear.

He still considers Macassar the best place for trade on the Islands. The king there is favourably disposed towards them. Unfortunately, Pessart has left a debt of 5500 reals, but Leyel hopes that he will soon be able to pay it off.

At Bantam the completely trustworthy Herman Clausen Rugmand had built up and organized the trading station after Claus Rytter had left him there for that purpose in March 1643. However, he became seriously ill and persuaded the Dutch governor at Batavia to permit a Dutch ship to transport him to Dansborg where he arrived on September 2, 1644. He died a few hours after his arrival, but managed to hand over the station's capital in money and silver amounting to 4000 pieces-of-eight which Claus Rytter had left with him.

The very next day his belongings were sold by auction in the usual manner, a certain sum being set aside for his fiancée, Maria Lopez, according to his wishes. His effects are said to have had a total value of a little over 10,000 pardous. Everything is carefully listed in the accounts, from which we can see that Leyel bought a good deal of silverware for the table: a gilt chocolate dish, 12 silver platters, 2 salt cellars, 2 cups, and a gilt cup. Jørgen Hansen's purchases are more practical: 1 musket, 1 dagger, 1 woollen shirt, 2 black shoelaces, and 5 collars. Herman Clausen was plainly a very well-to-do man just like Nicolaj Samson. It would seem that the employees must have had an opportunity to trade for their own benefit – a practice which, if not entirely legal, was still something generally accepted. At any rate Leyel himself seems to have done something similar, as will be apparent from a later chapter.

The accounts were kept very carefully in Tranquebar. Today we may be a bit startled to find that all the accounts have as their heading: "Laus

Deo (God be praised) in Tranquebar". Claus Rytter's journal begins in similar fashion: "Laus Deo. In the name of the Holy Trinity". They were well aware that the voyages were long and perilous, and that many lives were lost in the tropics.

We can gain a certain insight into the income from the import duties that were collected at Tranquebar in 1644. The daily income from the town itself was often only a few pardous. But the revenue from the ships was a good deal larger; for instance the customs paid on a cargo of arrack was 40 pardous; a Dutch ship with a load of 1654 pieces of linen had to pay 41 pardous, and an Indian Rama Pule's sloop setting off on a voyage to Malacca, also with a load of linen, had likewise to pay 37 pardous. The total income for July 1644 was 325 pardous, for August 564, for September 769, for October 739, and for November at the close of the season only 394 pardous; but taken by and large a fairly decent income. However, some years later the income has decreased noticeably, though these are the winter months so they can hardly be compared; in November 1647 only 66 pardous, in December 109, and in January 1648 only 163 pardous.

A few days after the death of Herman Clausen Leyel sailed with the *Fortuna* up to Emeldy to spend the winter there. Masulipatnam was still completely closed to the Danes, until they could pay their large debts to the merchants there.

Since the Bengalis would not accept his conditions Leyel intended to continue his privateering war. It was by far the best way to obtain money to bolster the Company's poor economy, and the risks were minimal. In order to have everything out in the open he issued a declaration of war written in Persian. In August the *Christianshavn*, captained by Jørgen Hansen Riber, and the *Valby*, commanded by Simon Jansen, were sent off to look for Bengali ships on the way home from Tenasserim, Pegu, and Achin. The Bengalis were tired of having their ships taken by the Danes and sued for peace. The threat from the privateers had had a disastrous effect on trade as the Bengali ships were afraid to leave harbour. Leyel was pleased with the overtures, but swore that he would make them pay at least 100,000 rigsdaler before he gave in. The ordinary seamen probably wanted to continue privateering, partly because it was exciting, partly because it brought them a handsome extra income in prize money, whereas they had little chance of making money in any other way.

In 1641 the local governor of Masulipatnam had forbidden the Dutch to sell their cloves and nutmeg, as the king wished to buy their entire stock and thus gain a monopoly on this trade in his kingdom so as to force the prices up. But the Dutch considered this an attack on their rights and retaliated by blockading the coast of Golconda and seizing all Moorish ships on the way home from Persia.

Thus the Danes were not the only ones to attack Indian shipping. However, Leyel's purpose with his privateering war was to force the Bengalis and the Great Mogul to render suitable compensation for the great losses the Company had suffered as a result of the hostile actions of the Bengali governors, most of all the wreck of the *Jupiter* in 1625. This had been partly caused by the fact that the local nabob had imprisoned the captain just as a storm blew up, so that the ship was wrecked because there were no experienced officers on board and nobody on shore offered any assistance. Then followed the wreck of the *Nightingale* in 1626, where the crew had been kept in prison by the local prince until a ransom of 20,000 rigsdaler was paid. There was also the destruction of the Pipeley station in 1641, and the wreck of the *St Jakob* which might possibly have been avoided if the governor of Pipeley had been willing to offer help, but he had merely watched the show and then confiscated the cargo – though Mourids Christensen who lived at Dansborg some thirty years later says it was the common practice if "a vessel runs aground on a reef or shoal and one cannot immediately get it off but must ask for assistance. If the authorities to which the country and the shoal belong are told they are allowed to keep the ship and its cargo, but the crew will be at liberty to depart". So the governor seems merely to have followed the common practice when he retained the cargo, but acted illegally when he demanded a ransom for the crew. These misfortunes had completely ruined the Company's economy, and from the Danish point of view it was not unreasonable to demand satisfaction.

At first glance it might seem a desperate undertaking for the tiny Danish Company with its diminutive fleet to start a war with the Bengalis. It was only possible because the Moguls had no fleet, and the Bengali trading vessels were no match for European guns and cannon. It soon became apparent that the Indian crews usually did not dare to fight but fled in their boats as soon as the Danes appeared. It would, indeed, have been a most one-sided fight.

But when the two sloops the *Valby* and the *Fortuna* were being used in this way Leyel lacked ships to carry on the Eastern trade which, together with the customs receipts from Tranquebar, was the only reliable income since no ships arrived from Denmark. So although there was much work to be done at Dansborg he was very keen on getting the Bengali vessel they had seized in February 1644 and named *The Little Elephant* made seaworthy. As mentioned above he had delegated this task to Hans Knudsen at Corengy. Already a week after gaining access to Dansborg he writes to Hans Knudsen that as soon as the vessel is ready to put to sea he is to sail to Ceylon to fetch the elephants that the king of Candy has promised the Danes. He asks Knudsen to procure thirty good seamen, preferably Christians; but if that is not possible, then Moors. He is not to risk putting in at Narsapur or Masulipatnam on his way south, but make straight for Tranquebar. And as it is imperative to keep the Bengalis ignorant as to the movements of the privateers, he writes: "Do not let the Moors or any others know that the 'Valby' is on its way there, so that they will not get any ideas." The letter ends with an admonition: "I hope you are behaving decently and helping each other, which I doubt not.... With this I commit you to the protection of the Almighty." And in the next line follows: "Let me know the price of cinnamon, what the price is of a bar."

Three weeks later he reports that the *Valby* is now ready to sail for Corengy. The captain, Simon Jansen, has been entrusted with 134 reals to cover Hans Knudsen's expenses, together with a quantity of rope made locally from coconut fibre, as well as blocks both for the standing and the running rigging on the captured ship all made by a local craftsman. Some pumps have also been included. And Knudsen is again warned against letting anybody know the *Valby*'s plans. The element of surprise is vital. The Bengalis must never have any knowledge of where the Danish ships are lurking. Leyel writes that he himself will soon follow with the *Fortuna* and expects to be able to sail together with *The Little Elephant* on a privateering voyage. "But let no man know of my coming. And when the 'Valby' sails, say it is going to Tranquebar."

When Leyel with the *Fortuna* finally arrived at Corengy in September 1644 he was greatly disappointed to find that *The Little Elephant* was still far from ready to sail. Hans Knudsen seems to have become so addicted to drink that he had neglected his work, and when Leyel upbraided him for having wasted so much time Knudsen used such language that Leyel decided to give the task to somebody else and take Knudsen on board "to prevent any further mischief". Knudsen seems to have been a regular drunkard, but apparently not without a certain charm. It is evident that Leyel liked him; that summer he had written a number of letters to him from Dansborg in an almost confidential tone. But Knudsen seems to have been a weak character, thus on the voyage to India he had been put in irons for six days in the *Christianshavn* because of drunkenness and neglecting his duty. That he was fond of the bottle is also clear from an amusing little note sent to Captain Jørgen Hansen on May 31, 1641, while the ship was still at Tenerife: "I beg you not to be angry with me because I am ashore for I am in good company and now we will drink to your health. God be with you."

The task of getting *The Little Elephant* ready to sail was entrusted to a couple of other men, and as they were somewhat inexperienced Leyel begged an acquaintance among the Dutch merchants to assist them. He was eager to leave with the *Fortuna*, as he had some goods on board that he expected to sell at a good profit and with this money he wanted to buy cloth for a trading voyage to the Islands.

Knudsen was not the only man to cause problems. Shortly before Leyel had left Dansborg he had had to assemble the council to pass sentence on a bosun from the *Christianshavn*. The matter in itself is of no great importance, but is probably typical of many similar cases. Erik Lauridsen Thorbeck had twice run from the ship, but had been caught both times. He admitted during his examination that there was no special reason for his first attempt, presumably he was just bored or was fed up with the service. But when "he now for a second time has absented himself without leave from His Majesty's service it was drink that had caused it, and also his quarrels and disagreements with some of the crew of the 'Christianshavn'".

He now begged forgiveness for his wrongdoing; but the court martial feared it would lead to the breakdown of discipline and decided that he be keelhauled, flogged at the gangway and made to run the gauntlet. But with the addition that if he ran a third time he would be punished by death. There were so few Danish seamen that one hesitated to use the death penalty laid down in Christian IV's articles for men who ran from the service.

The privateering continued. When Leyel put to sea with the *Fortuna* he had the good luck to take a large Bengali ship of 720 tons on its way from the Maldive Islands with coconut fibre and the shells called cowries which from ancient times had been used as jewellery and a local currency. When the Indian skipper, the nakoda, saw that resistance was useless he and his men jumped into a boat with some ambergris and other valuables. He also took the sails, presumably in the hope that the Danes would then find it impossible to remove the ship.

The Danes did manage to rig new sails, but the ship sailed very slowly, so Leyel sailed ahead to Emeldy, where he arrived all of a fortnight before the captured vessel, which was now made a part of the Danish fleet, and since it had been seized on St Michael's Day, September 29, it was named the *St Michael*. The cowries were sold for 3000 rigsdaler a sum that shows how much money the privateering ventures could supply. No wonder that Leyel, now that the Company was so strained financially, found this an easy solution.

The only other prize was an old ship belonging to a couple of merchants in Balasore. It was on its way to Masulipatnam with a load of tobacco. A prize crew of six Danes was put on board and it was expected to keep company with the others. But that night, as so often before, a storm blew up and the vessel was dashed on the coast where it was wrecked. The six Danish sailors managed to get ashore; but their situation was extremely difficult. They were in a hostile country and could not expect a hospitable welcome from the Bengalis whose ships they had taken. All of that first day the Danes kept themselves hidden in a forest, and only when it was completely dark did they dare to trudge towards the north, where they tried to aim for the mouth of the river near Pipeley. After many hardships they reached the swamps near the river and caught sight of the Dutch ship, the *Lys* lying at anchor. That evening they risked going down to the river bank and shouted for help. The Dutch then sent a boat to pick them up and promised to take them out to the *Christianshavn* which was anchored a little way off.

But nothing was done; and when the local governor soon after heard who they were and where they were he demanded that they be handed over. The Dutch, who were desirous of preserving their good relations with the Bengalis, then handed over the six Danes to their fate. They were chained hand and foot and taken to a prison in the town. The plan was the next day to take them inland to the prince of Bengal who was the son of the Mogul. He would know how to find a suitable method of revenging the many acts of piracy.

But it so happened that very evening that a boat was sent ashore from the *Christianshavn*, where nobody had any idea of the fate of the six Danes, to fetch fresh water and wood. On its way back just before it was dark the boat passed close by the *Lys*. The men paused to talk with the Dutch and heard for the first time that not only were the six men still alive, but that they had just been handed over to the Bengalis. The Danes were naturally furious with the Dutch and used strong language.

But as they rowed on the crew spoke eagerly of rescuing their comrades and with some difficulty they persuaded Carsten Ludvigsen, who was mate on the *Christianshavn* and Poul Nielsen, the merchant, who were both in the barge to attempt a rescue. The latter proved an invaluable leader as, from his former service at the Danish station at Pipeley, he was familiar with the whole district.

The small force consisting of the two officers, eight Danish seamen, and seven men from Tranquebar now hid themselves on the bank of the river at some distance from the town. At midnight, when all was still, they rowed silently in to Pipeley. Poul Nielsen was able to lead them straight to the governor's house, where they supposed that the prisoners were being held. Armed with pistols, swords, and axes the Danes suddenly rushed out with loud shouts, attacked the guards at the gate and shot several of them. The Bengalis panicked and ran aimlessly about shouting "The Danes! The Danes!" In the confusion the governor escaped out of the back door, mounted his horse and galloped off. Apparently the Danes met little resistance and speedily searched the house, but could not find their comrades.

Poul Nielsen then said that there was another possibility. The prisoners might have been taken to the town hall where one of the rooms was sometimes used as a prison. So they hurried there. The house proved to be guarded by a number of soldiers who had heard the shots fired at the governor's residence and stood ready with naked daggers. There was a short, but violent fight and several of the guards were killed, while the rest ran away. The Danes now dicovered that the gates were locked, but as they still held the axes they had had with them to chop wood it did not take long to force their way in. Great was their joy when they found their six comrades all safe. But now there was a new problem. The heavy iron chains around their legs meant that the prisoners could not run down to the barge and had to be carried through the town. Everywhere shouts and alarm signals were to be heard, drums were beaten, people ran about the streets with flaming torches, riders on horseback seemed to be everywhere, and soon arrows and musket balls whistled about their ears. However, they all made it down to the riverside, jumped into their boat and rowed hastily away from the enraged town. At dawn they reached the *Christianshavn* in safety and could now take their time in filing the chains off their comrades. It turned out that nobody had been badly hurt. Only one man had a swordcut to his shoulder, while another had had an arrow shot through his hand; but they had got off lightly.

If privateering did not bring in enough money Leyel had thought of other ways of increasing his income. That autumn he sent the *Valby* to patrol the waters between Ceylon and Tranquebar and persuade the Indian sampans that came north loaded with goods not to continue towards Porto Novo. Instead they were to unload and sell their goods at Tranquebar. This would naturally result in a substantial increase in the customs receipts and would allow commerce at Tranquebar to flourish. Leyel was not the only one to have come up with this idea: both the Portuguese and the Dutch made use of a similar strategy.

Leyel also tried reaching accommodations with local Indian vessels, one of which was "Anina's sloop". It was owned by an Indian merchant Anina at Tranquebar, and Leyel had had plans of buying it. Later he seems to have entered into a partnership with Anina, as they both paid for the fitting out; but it seems as though much of the financing of the voyage was on his own, not the Company's, account. One should not underestimate the Asian vessels. Some of the Indian sampans were fairly large; thus there is mention of two ships with all of twenty-three elephants on board, and the ships sailed both to Persia and the East Indies. These were the freighters but, especially on the Islands, there were swift small vessels, catamarans, that with a good wind could sail as fast as twelve knots, far more than any European ship of this period. The first descriptions and drawings of the East Indian praus portray large canoes with a great sense of form and refined ornamentation. It must be remembered that the Arabs, Chinese, and the inhabitants of the East Indies had sailed in these waters for at least a thousand years before the Europeans arrived.

In July 1644 Anina's sloop with sergeant Adrian Jacobsen as skipper was sent to Cotiari in Ceylon with a supply of gifts for the king of Candy, from whom Leyel hoped to gain permission to trade without paying customs. The archives contain a detailed list of these gifts, showing the type of gifts one supposed would appeal to the king. There is a Japanese lacquered chest inlaid with mother-of-pearl, six bolts of valuable cloth of a type called pano rolado, a round mirror, two glasses with water and figures (whatever is meant by this), four bolts of red Tanjore cloth, a pound of camphor from Borneo, two small copper cannon, two Bengali hunting dogs, a falcon, two Malay monkeys, and an apparatus for distilling sea water. The accounts betray a little of the care needed to keep the gifts in good shape; it was not enough merely to buy them.

Paid 1 coolie who brought a falcon from Negapatnam	3 fano
1 silver ring to put around the falcon's leg	6 fano
1 silk cord for the above-mentioned falcon	4 fano
Chickens for the falcon's food	2½ fano
2 silk cords for the Malay monkeys	1 fano
Bananas for the monkeys' food on the voyage	½ fano
Medicine for the elephants	2½ fano.

Nevertheless, Adrian Jacobsen seems to have had difficulties in his nego-tiations for he was so slow in returning that Leyel began to get worried.

In October Leyel received a letter at Emeldy from Anders Nielsen at Dansborg. A sampan belonging to a citizen of Tranquebar had been on its way from Ceylon along the Indian coast when it was attacked by three vessels off Carical; they carried the sampan off with them and the owner complained to Anders Nielsen. In spite of the fact that Nielsen had no Danish vessel with which to pursue the troublemakers he at once set off in an Indian vessel with three white and three Indian soldiers – a somewhat inadequate force with which to punish the attackers. But apparently it was also a question of showing the flag: the Danes could simply not accept such treatment. However, the result was what might be expected: the same three ships came out and shot at them so that they had to return home. Nielsen then wrote a letter to the authorities at Carical threatening them with a day of reckoning as soon as one of the Danish sloops returned, when the Danes would retaliate by blockading the harbour, unless Carical at once returned the stolen sampan.

The adrigar of Carical replied that the year before the Danes had seized a sampan from them so that they had no reason to complain. They had merely wished to restore the balance. In his letter Anders Nielsen indignantly refutes this claim as pure nonsense. The sampan the adrigar may be thinking of was flying a Danish flag, and when a ship from Cari-cal demanded to see their pass, the Indian skipper went forward to show it. But then shots were fired without warning, the skipper was instantly killed, and two other members of the crew were wounded. But when the rest of the crew seized their weapons the Portuguese had sailed off and had probably also lost several men.

Anders Nielsen is also able to tell Leyel that Adrian Jacobsen has final-ly arrived home from Ceylon with Anina's sloop. He has concluded the desired trade agreement and also brings an elephant he has received as a gift from the king. Nielsen believes that the elephant can later be used as a gift to the nayak. It seems that Ceylonese elephants were especially prized by the Indian rajahs as being superior to the Indian ones. The Dutchman Linschoten writes: "They are considered the best in all India, and daily experience confirms the truth of this, as elephants from all other places and countries greet them and do them honour by bowing their neck between their forelegs." Nielsen admits that the elephant is somewhat emaciated after the voyage which had taken thirteen days, so that it will have to be fattened up before it can be used as a gift. He has also had problems housing it, as it is so tall (he gives its height as about 5 cubits (a cubit was between 18 and 22 inches)) that it could not enter the gate to the fortress, and Nielsen had to erect a separate house for it outside the walls.

Towards the end of the year Leyel receives a few more letters from Anders Nielsen, one of them with the joyful tidings that a couple of Danish ships from home are anchored at Cotiari in Ceylon. It is almost too good to be true – and so it was! The rumours were wholly without foundation.

The other letter tells how Dansborg is more or less under siege. On December 20, 1644, an Indian general from Tanjore had appeared at the head of a large army demanding that the inhabitants of Tranquebar give him 600 rigsdaler as a present. It turned out that the general's brother Regnapule had been given a lease of both Carical and the country south of Tanjore along the coast in return for which he was to pay the nayak 900,000 rigsdaler. In order to scrape together this enormous sum – and preferably a good deal more for himself, which was of course the main reason for concluding such a bargain – he had been given the right to levy a tax on the inhabitants on a scale he himself determined. But the nayak had long ago surrendered the right to tax Tranquebar to the Danes, so that the inhabitants naturally rejected the general's demands.

General Tiagepule then surrounded the town so that no goods could pass in or out. As this state of things could not be sustained for a longer period of time, Anders Nielsen, who seems to have been a resolute character, made a sortie with his men and drove the enemy troops away. A couple of days later, on Christmas Day, while all the Danes were attending the service in the church Tiagepule attacked the northern part of the town with his men, burned a number of houses and made off with a quantity of textiles belonging to the Company which the dhobis (washermen) had left near the river. Anders Nielsen remained in church until the sermon was over, but he then hastily collected some of the fortress's soldiers and drove Tiagepule's men away.

An elephant is presented to the king of Pegu in Burma. In the background the elephant greets the king by falling to its knees and lifting its trunk in salute. In the shed
the elephant is being washed by a servant. Note that the elephant, with no less than
eight servants to carry his canopy has jewels (?) in his ears, and elaborate patterns
carved in his tusks. (Joan Theodor de Bry: India Orientalis, Frankfurt 1598-1613.)

When the army launched a fresh attack during the night and burned a few more houses, Anders Nielsen collected a large company, and at dawn they joined battle which lasted for about three hours. Tiagepule lost seventeen men, while Anders Nielsen was the only man wounded on the Danish side when a bullet struck his left arm. They seem to have agreed to some kind of armistice until Leyel was home again and could decide the next step. There seem to have been no more skirmishes, but this may simply have been because the Danes had no more powder; at least on December 30 Anders Nielsen writes: "You should know that we have no more powder in store."

Leyel had enough worries and disappointments up north to contend with. Hans Knudsen had not been able to reconcile himself to his reduced rank and in a letter he begs Leyel "with sighs straight from my heart, entreaties, and petitions on bended knee" for forgiveness, because he had been drunk and not attended to his job; but Leyel would not relent. In the middle of October the *Fortuna* with the two men on board is back at Emeldy; but they discover that the goods Leyel had left here could not be sold, nor could they buy anything because the governor of Masulipatnam had forbidden all trade with the Danes: Leyel must come to Masulipatnam if he wishes to trade. But Leyel is sure that the Danish debts in that town amount to about 5500 reals, and remembering Claus Rytter's treatment he dares not enter the town. He is in fact so angry with the governor that he writes Anders Nielsen that he intends to seize two of the governor's ships as soon as they leave harbour. Rumour has it that one is planning to sail to Persia, the other to Mocha. Leyel will then remove from their cargo the textiles he has not been able to buy because of the governor's embargo, and then as an honest man pay for it all at the current price. But he may also demand damages for the loss the governor had caused Claus Rytter. A somewhat unique form of piracy!

There was nothing for it but to transfer most of the unsold goods to *The Little Elephant*, which was finally launched on November 6 and was now lying ready to sail in the roads. But on 9 and 10 of that month a hurricane blew up and the frigate drifted towards the shore. They tried to save it by cutting the masts to lessen the pressure of the wind and threw the cannon out as extra anchors, but it was all to no avail. The ship was cast up on the reef, where it was broken up by the waves. Most of the men were saved, but all the goods were lost. Leyel estimated the value at 5000 rigsdaler, another devastating catastrophe for the Company. Whether Hans Knudsen was in any way directly responsible for the wreck is not clear – but his tardiness had certainly delayed the ship's departure, and it is not unlikely that Leyel upbraided him with this. He seems to have felt himself to be guilty, for some days later he committed suicide by jumping overboard.

The *St Michael* was nearly wrecked in the same storm. They lost both anchors and drifted hopelessly towards the reef off Narsepur, where they were stranded. They cut the mainmast, and fortunately the wind shifted at the last moment so that the ship was saved.

Other ships had also been in difficulties during the storm. Two Moorish ships were said to have drifted from the roads off Emeldy so that one was stranded and was wrecked by the waves near Masulipatnam – it had a crew of sixty-four, seven of whom froze to death, while the others were saved. The other ship simply disappeared, presumably lost with all hands.

In early January 1645 Leyel sailed with the three Danish ships, the *Christianshavn*, the *Fortuna*, and the *St Michael*, from Emeldy where the ships had wintered. On board he had the remainder of the goods and some timber, which was more easily obtained in that region. They made for Tranquebar, but because of contrary winds did not arrive before the end of the month. The trade along the coast to the north had failed completely; the governor of Masulipatnam had now also forbidden the merchants at Emeldy to trade with Leyel. This had made it impossible to buy the essential cotton goods for sale on the Islands, and besides that, some of the textiles which had been stored at Tranquebar had been burned by Tiagepule's people. So Leyel felt they would have to give up sending ships to Bantam and Macassar that spring.

The *Christianshavn* now needed to be overhauled, and in February he sent it to the Dutch shipyard at Cotiari together with the *St Michael*. The shipworm had been busy, and the ship would have to be provided with new planks. The *Valby* was sent with Simon Jansen to Carical to revenge the above-mentioned attack on a sampan belonging to a citizen of Tranquebar. He seized two sampans lying in the roads; but unfortunately two Dutch ships lay at anchor there, the above-mentioned *Lys* and one other, and the crews entered the fray, boarded the *Valby* and took Simon Jansen back with them where they kept him prisoner for three to four hours, until the sampans he had seized had got to safety. It was also known that Carical had supported Tiagepule in his war on Tranquebar.

The third ship, the *Fortuna*, was sent with Anders Rudkøbing as master and a crew of two whites and a number of Indians with some goods to Galle in southern Ceylon. Nothing was heard of the ship for a long time, and Leyel began to fear that it had been lost; but it turned out that a storm had blown it off course and it had had to seek harbour at Queda on the Malay Peninsula, where he had succeeded in selling the cargo – a dangerous voyage that shows how difficult and unpredictable sailing in these waters could be. His stay there lasted three months, and when the ship finally reached home it, too, had to be sent to Cotiari for repairs.

Life was so full of problems that Leyel and the other leaders must often have felt that it was completely hopeless. They were constantly being reminded of the fatal lack of money and men. Sometimes they must have wondered why they kept going. If nobody at home was interested in Tranquebar it might perhaps be better to give up and go home.

There were always fresh problems. Leyel maintained that he had already paid Pessart's debts to the nayak of Tanjore – though it seems rather doubtful if this was the absolute truth. The nayak seems to have felt differently. At any rate, he now sent a message demanding that the Danes present him with gifts and suggested that a suitable gift would be goods to the value of 8-10,000 rigsdaler. Leyel could see no end to the calamities. There was not the slightest hope of raising that amount of cash. His anger at Berent Pessart flamed up again. Because of his incompetence Leyel dared not enter Masulipatnam – was this now to be true also of Tanjore? The nayak would be angry when he did not receive the present he had asked for – would Leyel be held prisoner if he ventured to go himself? The matter was debated by the council, and it was decided to send Anders Nielsen with the big elephant from Ceylon as a present together with some fine Chinese silks, some of the red cloth which was always in great demand, a large Venetian mirror, a couple of small copper cannon, a gold chain to the value of 211 pardous, 726 pounds of sandalwood and 50 bottles of rosewater – it was a modest gift, the value only about 3,000 rigsdaler, but hopefully enough to allay the nayak's anger. Antonio Pacheco was sent along with Nielsen as interpreter. When Leyel later described the events in a letter home he added in a jocular tone that the council had felt it was better to risk the egg than the hen – one could possibly manage without Anders Nielsen for a while, but Leyel would have been harder to replace.

But Leyel still held a trump up his sleeve – an unusually elegant palanquin or litter he had brought with him from Masulipatnam; it had to be repaired first, but then he intended to send it after Anders Nielsen who was to present it to the nayak. It must have been very impressive, and that is saying a good deal, for the Indian rajahs had palanquins that were veritable works of art.

Rumours of the wonderful new palanquin had apparently already reached Tanjore, for Anders Nielsen writes to Leyel immediately after his arrival in the town at the beginning of March that everyone is talking about it, and the nayak has asked several times whether it has not yet arrived. He asks Leyel to hurry its dispatch as much as possible, "for our business will not advance at all until it arrives".

At any rate, Anders Nielsen was given a kind reception and then ventured to advance the Danish complaints of Tiagepule's attacks and to ask for damages. The nayak replied that the Danish governor ought to come himself and negotiate. But Anders Nielsen said that Leyel was having trouble with his legs and could hardly walk, but he would come as soon as he was well. As to Leyel's sudden illness – this is the only time we hear of it – it may of course have been real enough, but it is perhaps not very likely.

The nayak seems to have asked Anders Nielsen to be patient a few days, then Tiagepule himself will arrive and the nayak will inquire as to the harm he has caused the Danes and pay the damages.

But the friendly atmosphere seems suddenly to have evaporated. Anders Nielsen asked in vain for an audience with the nayak; but rumour had it that the nayak had said that he would send to Regnapule and ask him to order his brother to leave Tranquebar alone.

The palanquin did at last arrive; but now Nielsen had no opportunity to present it, as the nayak was said to have left for a temple some distance away, and when he finally returned it was to present the Danes with an ultimatum. Anders Nielsen was summoned and told that the Danes must sign an agreement to pay the annual tribute as they had done in the former nayak's time, and also promise to assist the nayak in his wars at sea and on land wherever he wishes. At this period Tanjore was involved in a number of conflicts with the surrounding kingdoms.

Anders Nielsen was dismayed; he could not decide such matters on the spur of the moment. He said that this was a completely new demand, something the Danes had never been under any obligation to perform. But now the nayak became very angry. He was evidently furious and threatened the Danes with all sorts of reprisals if they did not sign. He would drive them out of his kingdom and never again allow them to set foot there.

Anders Nielsen begged humbly that the nayak would not be angry; he had no authority to reply to such a demand and they must have a little time to think the matter over; but when they had eaten he would give

The tower of the Brihadeshwara temple in Tanjore (now Thanjavur) built ca. AD 1000. The tower is ca. 230 feet and on its top lies a huge block of stone said to weigh eighty tons. The ramp used to set it in place is said to have been over six miles long. Tradition claims that the tower collapsed when the first attempt was made to place the huge stone. (Photo: Thorkild Græsholt, ca. 1955.)

144

his answer. He finally agreed to the nayak's demands, and in his report to Leyel he justifies this decision partly because the nayak had threatened to send his ships to Tranquebar, burn the town to the ground and demolish the fortress, partly with the fact that the nayak could simply arrest the whole delegation and then demand an exorbitant ransom. As far as he could see the reason for the nayak's sudden demand was that not only was he at war with his neighbours, but also with the Portuguese at Negapatnam, and so wanted the Danes' assistance, and probably most of all the use of the Danish ships and big guns.

On March 25 he could at last present the palanquin to the nayak who was much pleased with it and at once gave orders to prepare it for his next trip. Anders Nielsen had hoped that this would make it easy to solve all his problems; but instead there were new demands that the Danes must not improve the fortifications at Tranquebar and must immediately pay the usual tribute. It was rumoured that the nayak had been very angry and had threatened to drive the Danes out of Tranquebar and destroy the fortress. But a friend of the Danes had respectfully reminded him that in all the years the Danes had been in his kingdom they had never opposed him, but always been willing to serve him, and this had mollified the nayak. In spite of this Nielsen advises Leyel to strengthen his defences, but as quietly as possible so it will not be reported to Tanjore.

Anders Nielsen finally learned the real reason for the nayak's anger. About two and a half years ago, he had sent a messenger to Pessart asking him to come and pay the annual tribute. Pessart had not only refused to come, but had replied with the greatest scorn and contempt. When the poor messenger repeated this reply to the nayak the latter had refused to believe that any person in authority could use such language and he had had the messenger whipped for telling lies. Afterwards, however, he was convinced that the messenger had only told the truth, And as he believed that Pessart was still in command at Dansborg, his anger was easy to understand. Nielsen could only deplore the whole matter and tell him that Pessart had been removed as incompetent, and the Danes now had a new governor, Willem Leyel, whom the nayak may have known from his former visits to the country.

The atmosphere now changed completely and the nayak was all kindness. He had a letter written to Leyel on a silver plate promising to pay damages for the destruction caused by Tiagepule and reducing the annual rent from 3000 to 2000 pardous. "Your gifts have arrived safely and as I from this see your courtesy and loyalty to me … I promise you in return that you need not pay more than 2000 pardous a year as your tribute for Tranquebar" – a fine ending to Anders Nielsen's somewhat harrowing embassy.

The usual good relations with the nayak had been restored and to confirm this Leyel again sent Antonio Pacheco to the nayak with new presents – he could afford a little extravagance in view of the large re-duction of the annual tribute: some fine porcelain, sandalwood, a large gilt mirror, two parrots from Ternate, portraits of the Danish king and the heir presumptive, besides a large selection of exotic textiles, a cane of tortoise shell, and a writing set also of tortoise shell.

Leyel was quite content with the result of the mission. He calculated that the income from Tranquebar and the profit from the local Danish trade, which was exempt from customs duties, might amount to about 4000 rigsdaler annually. If from this sum the 2000 rigsdaler for the nayak were subtracted there was still a handsome profit, enough to cover the running of the fortress and the maintenance of the ships. Contrary to Pessart, who could see no advantage in keeping the place, Leyel felt that "Danisborgh is a good and profitable place, if everything is properly managed and the Dutch do not prevent us".

The last words are an allusion to the recent Dutch attempt to drive the Danes out of Tranquebar. They had secretly assisted Tiagepule in his attack on the town; but far more dangerous than this, they had sent a delegation with very valuable gifts to the nayak desiring him to let them have Tranquebar, and they naturally did not omit to point out that it would be far more advantageous to the nayak to have them as partners intead of the poverty-stricken Danes who always seemed to have bad luck, and who neither sent him the promised tribute or presents worthy of such a king. They pointed out that the Danish king now was a tired old man, who had more than enough problems in his own country and was so poor that he could no longer send ships to India.

It was a dangerous attack, and when Leyel heard of it he responded at once. With men he could trust he immediately sent the nayak the treaty his father Regnado had written on a long silver plate, in which he promised the Danes that no other European nation (apart from the Portuguese at Carical), no matter whether it be the Dutch, English, or French, should be allowed to trade in his country. As an honest man the nayak honoured his father's promise, and when he was reminded of the old treaty, he even refused to give the Dutch an audience, and they had to go home having failed in their mission.

The fear of the growing influence of the Dutch can be seen in many of Leyel's reports: "The Dutch will completely crush and destroy us".

Instead of the former trade with Masulipatnam, which was no longer possible, he discovered Porto Novo, where the Portuguese had had a trading station for 150 years. It was only seven miles north of Tranquebar. He found that here he could buy the textiles he needed for the lucrative trade with the Sunda Islands, and the linen was even cheaper. Masulipatnam had been a fine place when they had been able to sell cloves and sandalwood from the Islands at good prices and in their place buy cotton goods. But the Dutch had now obtained so great a monopoly on cloves that they could control the price, and this had fallen drastically. In Crappé's time one could sell 1 maen of cloves at Masulipatnam for 28 pieces-of-eight, and later for a number of years still get 20-24 before the price hit rock bottom, so that now the price was only 9-10 reals a maen, and as one had to pay 8-8½ reals at Macassar there was no longer any profit in that trade. Something similar was true of sandalwood. This was of course the reason why Pessart had been so eager to find new markets, but with little success. Porto Novo had the great advantage that the Dutch were forbidden to trade there, so that the Danes had a much larger scope.

But in March 1645 the Danes suffered a new calamity. Leyel had sent the barge off with the experienced mate from the *Christianshavn*, Carsten Ludvigsen, the man who had helped to free the six Danish seamen from the prison at Pipeley, together with five other Europeans to fetch some goods from the *Valby*. But the barge never returned, and they gradually came to realize that it must have sunk and Ludvigsen and the others had drowned.

A loss of six Europeans was a serious blow to the Company, and in his letters to the Company at home Leyel is constantly asking for more men. Indeed, he writes that he could not have managed if he had not been able to get men who had run from the English and the Dutch. In this connection he mentions two Englishmen, Thomas Wilson and Richard Hall, whom he had engaged in February 1645 during Tiagepule's siege of the town "to help defend the town Tranquebar from some robbers and bandits who came from the nayak of Tanjore to burn, rob, and steal from the inhabitants here". He engaged another three men for the defence of the town a week later.

Altogether it must be said that Leyel succeeded in maintaining excellent relations with both the English and the Portuguese. He seems to have been on familiar terms with the English captains and men from the trading stations round about. The English assisted him at Bantam where, after Herman Clausen's death, the Danes no longer had a trading station, and Leyel was on a friendly footing with the Portuguese viceroy Don Filip Mascarenhaes at Goa. This had meant that the Danes were given the freedom to trade at all Portuguese stations in India.

Adrian Jacobsen had come home from his embassy to the king of Candy with the good news that the Danes could trade anywhere in his kingdom without paying customs. Leyel reckoned that the value of this exemption was worth about 1000 rigsdaler a year, and in the following years the Danes traded more and more with Ceylon, something the citizens of Tranquebar had always done. It was by no means as long and dangerous a voyage as that to the Sunda Islands.

A significant portion of the "goods" that passed through Tranquebar consisted of slaves. Thus the accounts for 1647 show that in August of that year 8 slaves were exported; in September the number had risen to 165, in addition to the 193 slaves that were bought and sold locally; in October only 22 slaves were exported, while 20 were bought and sold.

It must be remembered that at that time the slave trade was widely accepted and by no means limited to European traders. Wealthy Persians, Arabs, and Indians had bought and sold slaves for centuries. The Danish Company had its own slaves; some of these were apparently skilled in various crafts, carpenters, masons, etc. And as far as one can see, it was customary for most Europeans to have at least one slave. Some apparently took such a servant home with them to Denmark. Thus Jon Olafsson tells of an Indian boy Catthay, later called Christian, whom his master had taken home to Denmark on one of the first ships. Even though such a servant had not been bought, the relationship was pretty much the same as between a slave and his master. Jon also mentions the said Catthay's brother (whose name was Agamemnon no less), who, though he was only eleven years old, served him well and faithfully. "God had given him a prepossessing appearance and a light skin. He sometimes asked me if he might go outside the gates in the evening to see the heathen festivals and the plays and games that are enacted there. He always knelt before me when he asked, and every evening he would come up to me, put my right hand on his head and asked me to give him my blessing." The boy's mother, who must have had a good opinion of Jon, sent her son over every Saturday all the year round with a brass box with sweet cakes. She asked Jon "to check and punish him as I thought best, teach him Christian manners and take him home with me to Denmark". As far as we know, Agamemnon did not come home with Jon; but that some others did so can be seen from the parish register of Holmens Kirke where the minister during Lent in 1633 baptized a son of "Ulrik Christian, the blackamoor or Indian, at the wheelwright's on Holmen" (Holmen was the Naval Yard). And in 1638 Frands Panirs was likewise baptized in the same place – he is described as Captain Ernst Pricker's blackamoor.

Leyel was himself involved in the slave trade. He apparently went into partnership with the aforementioned merchant Anina at Tranquebar. In September 1645 they fitted out the *St Michael* for a voyage to Queda with Simon Thorstensen as skipper. There exists a document showing that the freight on the goods on board is to be divided between them, so that Leyel pays one half and Anina the other. The goods are not specified, but listed as 128 large parcels, 8 small parcels, 9 pots, 3 chests, 2 canisters, and 114 slaves. The slaves had been purchased for 8 pardous a head, of which sum Anina had only paid a quarter. The sloop also had room for four passengers, each of whom paid 5 pardous for their passage. One could make a handsome profit by transporting slaves to the Sunda Islands and selling them there. Thus the Danish soldier Mourids Christensen states that in 1671 a healthy fellow, who might be bought on the Coast of Coromandel for 20 pardous might be sold at Bantam for 40 to 60 pardous, whereas a fine woman bought for 14 to 16 pardous sold for 20 to 30 pardous.

All this leads to the delicate question as to whether Company employees were allowed to trade for their own benefit. It was a problem the Dutch East India Company had struggled with for many years. Here each employee was permitted to bring home with him in his chest a moderate amount of Oriental goods of no great value. But this naturally led to smuggling. The temptation was enormous, and whom did it really harm if one managed a little trade on the side? The merchants and the officials had every possibility of manipulating the accounts, writing up the value of spoiled or stolen goods, putting their travel expenses too high, claiming percentages or accepting gifts from their trading partners, trading in the name of a local merchant – there was a wide range of possibilities, and everybody knew it. One may also ask how Herman Clausen had become so enormously rich. And a man like Nicolaj Samson is also said to have been wealthy. He must have been a rather exceptional case for when he had to leave Dansborg in 1644 all his goods were carefully listed and laid in a room with the doors and windows nailed tight. This may, however, have some connection with the fact that the English agent Francis Day on a former occasion had abducted his wife and goods in his absence. Roland Crappé must also have had a good sum tucked away when he went home – at least we know that he bought the big mansion in Gammel Strand in Copenhagen from the Company, and this must have cost a pretty penny.

To be sure, Leyel had formerly sworn that he would not himself take part in the Company's trade "unless he received permission thereto with the knowledge of the shareholders". But now that all connection with the Company in Copenhagen was severed it is easy to see that the temptation must have been enormous. Such trade was common in all the stations in the East. So it is likely that both Leyel and the others at this time did trade on their own account when the opportunity arose. It was desirable to provide something against a rainy day if one ever succeeded in getting back home to Denmark. There would not be any pension.

In late June 1645 Leyel appointed Nicolaj Samson skipper of the *Valby* and sent him to Porto Novo. The big Dutch three-master *Lys* tried to stop him on the way; but Samson was not one to give up easily, shot back at them and sailed on.

In spite of constant rumours of ships coming from home the sea off Dansborg's walls was as deserted as ever. Other ships anchored there; but the ships carrying fresh supplies, news, and money from home, so longingly awaited, never came. The days lengthened into months, and the months became years; the old ships became more and more battered and had constantly to be sent for repairs, and still one could only hope that tomorrow or next month or next year things might be different. The available men became fewer and fewer; Leyel had to see some of his most reliable men die off. How long could he keep things going without any assistance from home?

The privateering war had gradually harmed Bengali interests so much that the prince sent a Jesuit, Antonio Rodriguez, to Leyel to make a fresh attempt to reach a settlement. Leyel was requested to make an estimate of how much the Danes had lost through Bengali injustices, and he claimed a sum of 436,500 rigsdaler. But the Bengalis refused to accept this, finding it immensely exaggerated. They offered to pay damages to the amount of 80,000 rupees, but Leyel found this far too small a sum. The Bengalis then had to go back home to ask for new instructions, and Leyel agreed to suspend hostilities for the time being. But when the negotiations did not seem to lead to any result the privateering war was recommenced.

At Dansborg work progressed on the houses and the church. A number of windows and doors were still missing; but these were gradually being restored. When Pessart fled with *The Good Hope* he had removed all the iron he could find as it could fetch a good price. Indeed, he had been so eager that he had even removed the iron bars from the windows in the gatehouses, but these were now restored.

The fortifications were repaired. The northern redoubt was rebuilt with stones and mortar and topped with 13-feet tall breastworks, and the southern redoubt was also rebuilt and given a counterscarp on the outside of the wall and a fairly high palisade on top. The moats were cleaned out and were now about 42 feet broad and 12 feet deep. Finally, Leyel had erected a powder magazine outside the town where powder was manufactured according to a new system he had heard about. He reports enthusiastically that whereas twenty-four men formerly had to work with mortar and pestle to make 50 pounds a day, now fourteen men can make 170 pounds in the same period. Any powder they do not want themselves can easily be sold at Bantam or Macassar.

CHAPTER 11
THE LAST VOYAGES

It was now October 1645 and time to set off on the annual voyage to Bantam and Macassar, the voyages that were so vital to the Company's trade, not least during these years when there were no ships from Denmark. During the two years he had been in India Leyel had apparently, in spite of all the difficulties, gathered a store of the cotton goods that were in such high demand in the Islands, and these were now loaded on the *Christianshavn*.

Leyel decided to take Poul Hansen Korsør with him and leave him as manager of the important station at Macassar. Poul Nielsen was appointed interim governor at Dansborg, and the twenty-one men who were left to man the fortress had to swear allegiance to him before Leyel left: "Hereby we the undersigned swear that we will in every way acknowledge and respect the said Poul Nielsen as our leader and commander inside and without this fortress and be submissive and obedient to him". The oath also contains a passage to which Leyel understandably attached great importance: "We likewise swear that should Berent Pessart or any of his followers come here to this fortress or anywhere on the coast that we – in accordance with the said Commander's and His Majesty's Council's sentence and after the said Commander's instructions given to Señor Poul Nielsen – will not recognize the said Señor Berent Pessart as our governor, and still less allow him to govern or command either inside or without the fortress; but that each and all of us will do his utmost to restrain and arrest the said Berent Pessart and his followers." The document is duly signed by all the men in the fortress, though many were unable to write and have merely made their mark, and several of the signatures are very clumsy.

Leyel, who seems to have been a stickler for order, also had an inventory drawn up of everything of value in the fortress when it was entrusted to Poul Nielsen on October 18, 1645. It was probably all very correct, but hardly an act that endeared him to his men – most of them must have felt that it showed a lack of confidence, and what reason had Leyel to believe that a man such as Poul Nielsen was dishonest? It may be in this and similar decisions one can find the root of the discontent that was to blossom into full flower two years later.

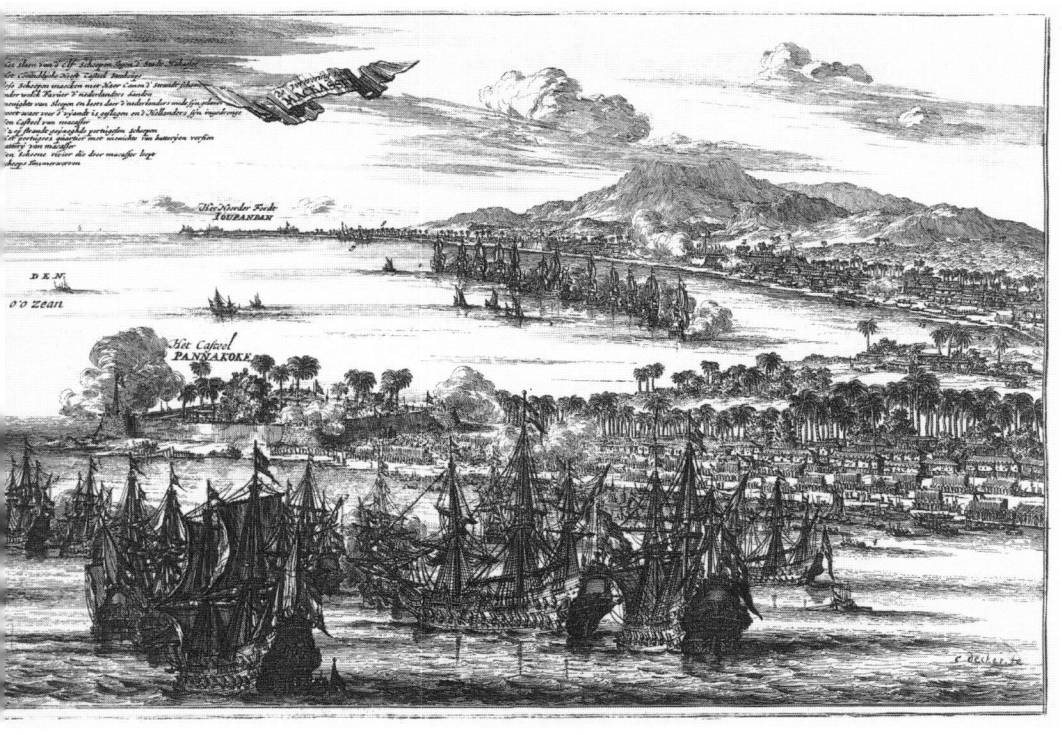

Macassar, the most important port on the island of Celebes, now Sulawesi. The Danish factory here was essential to all trade from Tranquebar. Danish ships called here frequently to sell cotton goods and slaves from the coast of India. Despite the Dutch prohibition it was possible to buy cloves, and these could be sold with a handsome profit both in India and of course in Denmark. (Walter Schouten: Ostindische Reyse, Amsterdam 1676.)

The inventory is of interest as it tells us something about how the fortress and Leyel's private apartment were furnished. For the running of the Company Leyel left 2000 rigsdaler, and in the storehouses lay 798 pounds of refined and 268 pounds of unrefined sulphur, 365 pounds of resin, 849 pounds of iron and 1275 pounds of coarse iron, 177 pounds of copper, 60 pounds of cinnamon, and 956 pounds of saltpetre.

In the commander's private apartment stood:
1 table with an ordinary painted table-cover
1 small table
1 bench belonging to the above large table
and in the bedchamber:
1 Danish table with a leaf.
In another chamber:
1 small table.

However, there must have been more furniture than the above, so this is probably only Leyel's own furniture, which he wished to make sure did not disappear while he was gone.

A curious object that is described as a "stone with its equipment for distilling water" is explained in Otto Sperling's "Notes de voyage en Espagne". On King Christian's orders Dr Sperling had accompanied Hannibal Sehested on his mission to Spain in 1640 when Sehested had saved the *Christianshavn* from the clutches of the Spaniards. In his book Sperling describes a device he had seen in Count Olivares' palace Buen Retiro. It consisted of three porous stones from the Canaries, set one above the other so that the Count's drinking water was filtered by dripping from one to the other. Sperling closes this passage with the words: "Three such stones were sent me by my good friend Willem Leyel from the Canaries to Copenhagen", and it seems likely that Leyel obtained a similar apparatus for his own use. Such filters have been used right up to our own times. Thus I remember from my childhood in India a similar device consisting of three large clay pots filled with sand, likewise positioned one above the other, so that the water was filtered through all three.

Of special interest is the list of Leyel's books, which gives us a glimpse of his intellectual make-up. Here is a sample:

Danish books:	Luther's catechism
	Jyske Lov (laws given by King Valdemar Sejr in 1241)
	Danmarks Riges Mønt (the Danish currency)
	Niels Michelsen's Medical Guide
Low Saxon books:	1 Gospel
	1 Augsburg Confession
	1 herbarium in folio
English books:	Purchas his Pilgrimes
Others:	A Malay and Portuguese dictionary compiled by Herman Clausen
	6 Moorish books (Arabic?)
	Persian books
Dutch books:	Plinius the Younger
	Historie Justinie
	Ovid's Metamorphoses

A collection that tells us something of his intellectual interests and familiarity with many languages. He seems to have been able to read Latin, was interested in botany, and probably spoke German, Dutch, Spanish, Portuguese, and Persian, possibly also Arabic, and to judge from his pleasure in the company of English captains and ownership of Purchas (which is a description of various voyages in English) probably English. A man so able in many languages must probably also have learned something of the local languages, especially Tamil, the language spoken around Tranquebar.

Leyel also had a copy made of the Articles given him by Christian IV before his departure and left it for Poul Nielsen together with his own instructions so that Poul Nielsen knew what was expected of him.

There is one more list dated October 5, 1645, of the things Leyel removed from the armoury for use on his voyage to Macassar. Chief among these were a number of different charts of the Coast of Coromandel, Sumatra, Java, Celebes, and all the way up to Japan and the coast of China; 2 minute glasses, 4 brass dividers, 3 compasses, 1 Spiegel der Seefahrt, a little box with instruments, copper wire, pincers, etc. Apparently he did not ordinarily have access to these things for he notes that they are taken from the deceased Carsten Ludvigsen's chest, should anybody put forward a claim to his property.

Now that everything was in order at Dansborg, Leyel sailed from Tranquebar on October 20, 1645, towards Bantam and Macassar in the hope that the trade would "make it possible for him to pay off all the debts Berent Pessart had contracted many years ago at Macassar". He even hopes that he can make a sizable profit, he dreams of 25,000 rigsdaler, but this is probably optimistic.

On December 12 the *Christianshavn* lay anchored off Bantam. The town was protected towards the sea by a massive high wall of blocks of white coral with many redoubts and with cannon distributed along it. The houses were not very impressive for, on account of the frequent earthquakes, most were built of bamboo. A river ran through the middle of the town and divided into two channels. The bazaar where gold, silver, and precious stones were sold lay on the outskirts of the town to the east, whereas the English and Dutch stations were to the west near the Chinese quarter, for there were many Chinese merchants. The surrounding country was very beautiful with mountains, woods, and cultivated fields, and everywhere a profusion of the vividly coloured tropical flowers and quantities of delicious juicy fruit.

The prince of Bantam always appeared in public with a magnificent display. He owned an impressive large canoe or prau embellished with elaborate carvings in which the prince could sit back under a scarlet awning to protect him from the burning sun, while the many rowers propelled it with their paddles. The carvings were further decorated with inlaid gold and silver so they glistened in the sun. Wherever he went his servants held a magnificent parasol over him of white embroidered damask with three golden crowns on top. And both inside his palace and outside he was accompanied by his royal guard in colourful costume and armed with muskets, spears, and sabres, and by musicians playing drums, flutes, and stringed instruments. At their festivals the dancing-girls appeared in glittering costumes and moved in time to the music with graceful gestures.

When visiting the local merchants Leyel was treated to "brum", the local alcoholic drink, made from fermented rice, coconut milk, and brown sugar. It was generally served together with fruit and jam in porcelain dishes. The Chinese always served tea, which was still an unknown beverage in Europe.

From Bantam Leyel sent a report home to the Company relating all that had happened, for here at last was a chance to send a letter home by an English ship.

His report is not without self-importance: "If we had not arrived in India with the ship *Christianshavn* and ordered all things in the way it has been accomplished both the fortress and all else had been lost." But

XXXII.
ACCVRATA DESIGNATIO BAZAR SIVE FORI IN
BANTAM, CVM SVIS MERCIBVS, 26.

Orum in Bantam ita constitutum est. A. Locus, quo Melones, cucumeres, & cocus venduntur. B. Locus vendendo saccharo, & melli destinatus. C. Fa-
barum forum. D. Statio Bambi, seu cannarum saccharearum exponendarum. E. Locus, quo pugiones, Cris, Acinaces, hasta, & arma catera emuntur. F. Li-
neos pannos viri. G. eosdem foeminae vendunt. H. Officina aromataria. I. Bengalorum, sive Gussaratarum taberna ferramentaria. K. Chinensium taber-
na. M. Forum piscatorium. N. Forum pomarium. O. Forum olitorium. P. Forum piperis. Q. Forum caparum. R. Forum oryza. S. Ambulacrum merca-
torum. T. Gemmariorum taberna. V. Nauicula, aliunde victualia conuehentes. X. Forum gallinarium.

i 2

A bazaar in Bantam. Much of the trade was carried on in such markets all over the
East Indies. At A women are selling melons, cucumbers and coconuts, at B sugar, at C
beans, at D sugarcane, at E weapons, at F-G cloth, at H spices, at I-K Bengalese and
Chinese food, at M fish, N fruit, O vegetables, P pepper, Q onions, R rice and at X
poultry. (Joan Theodor de Bry: India Orientalis, Frankfurt 1598–1613.)

this was probably true enough. He goes on to tell how they have not received any letters from home for several years, neither Leyel nor any of the others have had news of their families in Denmark and many suffer from homesickness. This gives rise to unrest, and Leyel admits that he never feels "safe from rebellion and other dangers, which we now fear, and which may arise from the long and tiresome service" the men have to endure and which seems to have no end. The leaders must constantly be on guard and keep a watchful eye on the men; there had been an open mutiny led by the two clergymen, and it could easily happen again, for – as Leyel puts it – "from a small spark can follow a great fire".

Leyel had already been three weeks in Bantam, but the trade was far from satisfactory as both the Dutch and the English had large stores of the same textiles he was trying to sell. In order to save Leyel had decided to close the Danish station here at Bantam and sell the house, as it cost quite a lot: 180 reals in annual rent to the king, besides the obligatory presents, which Leyel estimated at 500 rigsdaler a year.

In his letter to the Company Leyel also suggested that other nations be given permission to sail under the Danish king's pass and with Dansborg as a base for their trade, for which they should be made to pay a certain fixed sum to the Company. In this way Tranquebar could become an important centre of trade in the region, it would be of great advantage to the Danes, and bring in a handsome profit. Yet more proof of Leyel's indefatigable desire to promote the Company's interests. If only he could have had the necessary support he might have gone far. But conditions at home were hopeless, the king was old, and had practically given up the struggle.

On February 4 the *Christianshavn* arrived at Macassar and stayed there until well into June. Poul Hansen was now made manager of the station, which had had no leader since Herman Clausen had returned to Tranquebar in the autumn of 1644 only to die soon after his arrival there. Trade was no more lively here. Before he left Leyel deposited goods worth 2277 pardous, which he had been unable to sell. And it was during his stay here that Leyel received the letter from Berent Pessart's unhappy crew, now serving as slaves on the Spanish galleys at Manila.

At the same time Leyel seems to have heard so much about how profitable trade with the Philippines could be that he wrote home saying that it might be well worth trying. The Spaniards sent large quantities of textiles, silk, damask, satin, and linen, spices, silver, precious stones, and pearls from Manila to Mexico, from where the goods were sent by packtrains of mules across the Panama Isthmus and were then sent home to Spain. He has heard of profits up to 400 per cent, a result which must make a thrifty Danish merchant eager to obtain a share. So Leyel suggested that King Christian ask the Spanish king for permission to participate in the trade with the Philippines since the Danes had recently concluded a treaty of friendship with Spain.

The *Christianshavn* continued to Charabon on Java where the prince was very friendly to the Danes, promised them freedom from customs duties and promised Leyel to obtain pepper and other goods for him. It was a busy centre for trade and Leyel considered opening a station here. Another good place for trade was Japara; but as usual all plans of expanding the Company's business were blocked by the constant lack of men.

By early August the *Christianshavn* was at Batavia, where a Malay called Chinena Chetty, who probably knew Leyel from his former stay in the town when he was in the service of the Dutch East India Company, had asked the Dutch council if Leyel might represent him at a judicial dispute between him and the Dutch; the proceedings continued for six days, but Leyel felt that the Dutch were not receptive to arguments. They had the power and meant to use it. He also felt the same way about their attitude to Danish complaints.

And the Danes felt that there was plenty to complain about in the way the Dutch treated them. Though they had no right to do so they had demanded customs of two Danish ships sent to Queda in 1645 to trade there – the Portuguese had never demanded customs. And now when Leyel inquired at Batavia the Dutch forbade him to trade in Japan, on the Chinese coast, or on the coast of Sumatra. They especially wanted to keep traders out of Japan, for – as Leyel puts it – Japan was "the heart's blood in their body". So it was not without reason when he wrote "The Dutch are always in our way, hindering us" and he estimates that they have caused damage to Danish trade amounting to "several casks of gold". Here at Batavia Leyel tried to procure some equipment for the *Christianshavn* that he had not been able to get elsewhere. But some of these things were not to be had here either, as the Dutch had received no supplies at all from Holland that year. But for once a kind Dutchman found him a bookkeeper and a barber or surgeon – *Christianshavn*'s barber had gone with Pessart – and promised to try to procure the other things next time there was a ship from home. He also promised Leyel that if it was at all possible he would send him fifteen or sixteen Danish seamen from ships that called at Batavia.

On September 3, 1646, the *Christianshavn* was back at Tranquebar. Here there was once again a bad famine. The price of rice was twenty-eight times as much as before, and hundreds of thousands had died or sold themselves as slaves. To be sure, some rain had now fallen, and the rice fields looked promising; but the country was almost empty of people and there were far too few to bring in the harvest. In order to procure rice Leyel sent the *Fortuna* and the *Valby* to Ceylon, where the king of Candy got them what they needed. The *Valby* returned safely to Tranquebar before the monsoon. But the *Fortuna* had remained at Cotiari although the ship had a good load of cloves on board. The reason given by the inexperienced skipper Anders Rudkøbing was that he had not been able to get sufficient ballast for the ship — or was this merely an excuse? Leyel was frustrated at having to trust a ship to such an idiot: "as if there were not stones enough at Cotiari". "God help me when one has to rely on such inexperienced men!"

A fortnight after Leyel was back at Tranquebar he sent the *Valby* with Simon Jansen as skipper on a piratical voyage along the coast of Bengal together with the *Christianshavn* that now had a crew of 100, most of them lascars, with Jørgen Hansen as captain and Poul Nielsen as merchant "to attack and take as many Bengali ships as you can find there". Leyel impressed on them the necessity of keeping their movements secret: "If you have taken a prize don't let it seek harbour anywhere, but send it straight here. And when the *Christianshavn* reaches Masulipatnam and you have a prize with you then don't let it enter the roads there, but send it straight here".

But the idea of concluding a peace with the Bengalis continued to raise its head and according to Leyel's instructions Jørgen Hansen went to Balasore to get the matter settled; but he felt that the governor was not interested, so he abandoned the idea and sailed off on a new privateering voyage. This time they took a number of good prizes, possibly because the Bengali merchants thought that a peace had been concluded and so had left their safe harbours. In late January 1647 they took two ships, one belonging to the Great Mogul Shah Jahan himself, the other to Merse Meliquebak, the governor of Balasore. A little later they seized a large sloop with a load of 1030 maus of rice and 300,000 arrow shafts, and after that a couple of small vessels with another 1000 maus of rice. Two of the captured vesels seem to have been on a trading voyage to Ceylon and the other two were similarly aiming for another destination. Several of the captured guns were placed on the walls of Dansborg in place of those Pessart had stolen.

At about the same time Leyel sent Frantz Erkmand with the *St Michael* to Queda with a shopping list that included six elephants, pepper, gold, and fifty to sixty bar of resin. But Erkmand never reached Queda; the ship was beaten off course to the Andaman Islands, a group of islands whose inhabitants were known to be cannibals, and several members of the crew were killed – and probably eaten.

There was still no ship from Denmark, and the years gradually reduced the number of men. Adrian Jacobsen had died in 1646, and in late January 1647 Poul Nielsen died shortly after his return to Tranquebar of an illness that only lasted forty hours.

It is even possible to gain a picture of the common seaman's death. In May 1647 the *Christianshavn* is anchored at Cotiari, and on the orlop deck one of the Danish seamen lies dying. The mate Nicolaj Samson is summoned so that he can write the dying man's last will. It reads: "In the name of Jesus Christ, Amen. I, Albert Madsen, born on the island of Ærø in a town called Ærøskøbing, my father named Mads Elbertsen, my mother named Anne Jacobsdatter. Since the Almighty God of Heaven now has stretched me on this my sickbed, and with his Fatherly hand laid on me this illness, and I find myself admonished by the same illness, and I am sure that death is certain, but the time of death uncertain, I have resolved thus, being, God be praised, of a sound mind: First of all give to the poor of the wages I have earned 40 pieces of eight. Next, to my dear parents of the remaining money, if they be still alive, but if they be not alive then to my sister and brother. If they are not alive then to my nearest relative who is then alive. As to my clothes that are here on board that they may be given to him who has nursed me in my illness. I humbly beg my officers that all this may be done. Actum in East India in His Majesty's ship *Christianshavn* in the Bay of Cotiari, May 24, 1647." The will is duly witnessed by Jørgen Hansen, Niels Samson, and Amund Olufsen; but it is not very likely that his relatives benefited greatly from his will.

It is strangely moving to sit with a parcel of these carefully preserved testaments in one's hand. The bundle from Claus Rytter's *The Gilded Sun* consists of forty-five wills – a silent witness to the many poor devils who breathed their last on the murky lower decks far away from home. Their last wishes were carefully recorded on the papers, and maybe it is a little comfort to know that the captain or mate sat by their side long enough to write their last will. Others, who had nothing to bequeath probably left no testament, while still others died so suddenly that it was impossible; so the number of deaths must have been much higher.

But however many died, the trade must continue unless they were to abandon Dansborg. There were still not enough ships to carry on the vital trade on the various routes along the coast, to Ceylon, to Queda, and the East Indian Islands. This was why Leyel in 1646 asked Anders Nielsen to buy an Indian vessel of 240 tons. It was given the name *St Peter and St Paul* and cost 1600 pardous. It was immediately employed in the local coastal trade and continued here for the rest of Leyel's governorship.

Although the new sloop was quite a large ship there were only four Danes on board. Besides the skipper Simon Jansen and Anders Nielsen there was a mate and an assistant; the rest of the crew consisted of three boatswains, possibly Dutchmen, and a clerk Antonio Correro, to judge from his name a Portuguese; an Indian carpenter called Bartholomeo, who was a slave of the Danes, another Indian carpenter, and eight lascars.

On February 1, 1647, *St Peter and St Paul* sailed on a trading voyage to the Islands along the usual route to Bantam, Cherabon, Japara, and Macassar. On board were goods valued at 2341 pardous. Leyel had made out a shopping list of things they lacked at Tranquebar hoping that Anders Nielsen as the ship's merchant would be able to obtain them either at Batavia or in some other place. Among other things he lists 23-24 reams of good paper, 6 casks of tar, 8-10 cables for the sloops (2, 2½, 3, 3½ and 4 inches thick), 1750 gallons of arrack, 6 piculs of fine sugar as well as sugar to use for brewing beer for the fort, all sorts of rare textiles to be used as presents, 30 bar of lead, 3-4 small 2-3 pound cannon, timber, and Chinese textiles.

For once we get a glimpse of how much of the buying and selling was done. According to his instructions Anders Nielsen was first to negotiate with the Danes' local contact at Bantam, the Chinese merchant Ziu Ziu, who was to be allowed to buy whatever he wanted of the ship's cargo for cash, and as he was evidently considered completely trustworthy he could buy 500 reals worth on credit until the ship called in again on its way home from Macassar. After him the other merchants could buy whatever they wished, but only for ready money or on rendering security. At Cherabon there was a Javanese merchant who owed 620 reals from the previous year – he could of course not be allowed to buy anything till the debt was paid.

Among the goods Anders Nielsen bought at Bantam he mentions carpenter's tools, timber, bamboo, tar, arrack, sea charts, knives, iron pans, and Chinese birds' nests, known to be a great delicacy; all in all his return cargo cost 6840 reals.

After Poul Nielsen's death Leyel has nobody to take over the command at Dansborg when he is away; he therefore makes the disastrous decision to send for Poul Hansen. Anders Nielsen had with him a letter to Hansen at Macassar: "As Almighty God has called the late Poul Nielsen, merchant, home, and I lack persons here to whom I can entrust the fortress, should I travel to any other part of these countries, it is necessary that you and Joel Poelmand leave and come here with this sloop and do not leave any of our people behind." Before Poul Hansen leaves he should find a reliable man who can look after the station. And if Anders Nielsen is prevented from coming to Macassar with the sloop Poul Hansen must find an English, Portuguese, or – if need be – a Dutch ship that can bring him to Tranquebar.

On his voyage to the Sunda Islands Simon Jansen had seized a heavily laden Moorish ship and according to rumour killed the entire crew. In other words the Danes simply acted as pirates, and pirates have never been squeamish. Simon Jansen's excuse would presumably have been that there were too few men on board his ship to guard the prisoners.

At the same time that the *St Peter and St Paul* sailed to the Sunda Islands Nicolaj Samson was sent to Ceylon as an emissary to the king of Candy with expensive gifts, among other things four horses bought on the Sunda Islands, twelve Javanese lances, the blades of which were inlaid with gold, a Javanese kris or dagger with a hilt of gold and the blade inlaid with gold, a painted tent, three yards of red scarlet cloth and nine yards of broad gold lace.

In Ceylon Samson is to contact the Danes' local "consul", a man called Chedam Bernardo who lives there and will help him. As a return cargo he is to buy rice, 100 bar of wax, cinnamon and – as always – elephants. However, the voyage proved abortive, as the Portuguese prevented Samson from reaching Candy and he had to return having failed in his mission.

How large the Danish fleet was in late 1647 is not clear. Anina's sloop had been sold; but in October there is mention of *The Bengali Prize* with Willum and Oluf on board, and another prize with Christen Clausen and Cleen on board.

A hint that the Danes had by no means stopped their piratical expeditions can be seen from an English report from Bengal in late December 1647. Here we are told that an English vessel at this time was given a good reception at Balasore; but when a Danish fleet of five ships (*Christianshavn* must have been one of them) appeared and seized one of the

Moors' ships with eight elephants on board there was an abrupt change of mood. The Englishmen were asked to go to the Danes and persuade them to hand over the ship; but when this failed the Moors insisted that since both the English and the Danes are Christians the English must be held responsible for any damage caused by the Danes. The English then tried to escape with their ship; but the Indians blockaded the harbour, placed guns at strategic points and summoned large forces of soldiers. This led to a full-blown battle, but by this time the Danes had presumably already managed to bring themselves and their prize to safety.

At Tranquebar there were no letters from home; but in the course of 1647 Leyel did receive letters from his son Hans and Hans' English wife Eleanor. As mentioned earlier Hans Leyel had served as assistant on board Claus Rytter's ship *The Gilded Sun* when it left Tranquebar and can now tell his father the sad ending to that voyage at Portsmouth where the English authorities had confiscated both ship and cargo as compensation for the ships impounded by Christian IV. Hans and the other members of the crew did not receive a penny of their hard earned wages until twenty months after the ship had reached harbour. The case had ended by the authorities granting £500 en bloc to the whole crew; but from this sum they deducted the maintenance of the crew for the whole period, so that in the end Hans had received the princely sum of 2 pounds sterling. A dismal end to his voyage, for like most of the others he had hoped for a good profit from the goods he had brought home with him, but these had all been confiscated. So that the £2 was the meagre result of five years' hard labour.

Hans Leyel writes that he was ashamed to go home to Denmark without even a decent set of clothes and decided instead to seek his fortune in England, where he found employment with a merchant, a Mr William Stroud, and was gradually so highly esteemed by him that he gave him his daughter in marriage together with a dowry of £200.

Fortune seemed to smile on the young couple. But times were hard in England. King and Parliament were locked in a Civil War, and Hans was forced to enlist; but the young couple decided to buy another man to take his place and spent most of Eleanor's dowry to pay him. This meant that they only had the income from their house and farm to live on, about £6 a year. So Hans went to London to find work, while his wife remained with their little daughter at her parents' home at Winealton in Somerset. But there was fighting in that district, and one day a band of soldiers forced their way into the house and shot Eleanor both through her arm and through her body, and the family had to pay large sums for doctors and medicine before she was well again.

At the end of the letter Hans tells his father a little about conditions at home. All three of Leyel's co-directors of the Company, Johan Braëm, Jakob Mikkelsen, and Roland Crappé have died. But he has heard that King Christian has decided to establish a new East India Company as soon as his son-in-law Corfitz Ulfeldt returns from his journey to the Netherlands, France, and England, and next year they plan to send three ships to Tranquebar. The family news is not good: Leyel's wife Alhed or Alhel "is still alive and living at Elsinore at the carpenter's (probably the husband of Leyel's sister Dorete), but she is thoroughly demoralized, has wasted all her money on drink and tobacco".

He begs his father for financial assistance, and Eleanor also writes touching letters to her unknown father-in-law asking for help. Not very encouraging letters for Leyel to receive far away in India where he felt helpless because of his position. His wife was apparently living in degradation. His stay away from home had become so much longer than anybody could have dreamed. Who could have imagined that it would be nine or ten years, or perhaps even longer, before he could come home? The return voyage to Tranquebar had often only taken two years.

It seems as though communications with Denmark had failed completely; at any rate we cannot see from the preserved documents that any letter from the Company directors arrived at any time during this period and presumably there was as little news of family and friends. The feeling of isolation must have been oppressive.

But if Leyel had received letters from home, they would not have been very encouraging. His mother, Ingeborg Frederiksdatter, was still alive. But there was bad news about his sister Kirstine. Her husband, the highly gifted Morten Madsen had had an eminently successful career. He was the son of a baker, had studied at the University and taken a doctor's degree in theology. Christian IV had appointed him his personal chaplain at the castle of Frederiksborg and later still he became bishop of Aarhus. As a young man he had tutored the King's children by Kirsten Munk.

With his wife Morten Madsen had a quiverful of gifted young sons and daughters, and everything seemed promising. But unfortunately Morten Madsen quarrelled with the lord lieutenant Erik Grubbe of Tjele (father to Marie Grubbe, known from Danish literature) and with his sexton who considered himself an important and learned man, as he was both a printer and a writer and had edited a collection of old Danish proverbs.

This man had already held his post a long time when Morten Madsen was appointed bishop. Nobody knows what the quarrel was all about, but in 1641 there was a crisis, and the bishop simply fired him.

Among the bishop's daughters was one called Abelone, and that same year she married Pastor Christian Nielsen Bonde in Aarhus. Soon afterwards the sexton accused this clergyman of having an illicit relationship with his mother-in-law, and things became even worse when a fetus was discovered hidden in the churchyard belonging to Aarhus cathedral. It was the duty of the lord lieutenant Erik Grubbe to investigate the case, and there was a lot of gossip about the bishop's wife and her son-in-law. Poor Kirstine was accused of witchcraft, adultery, and the murder of her child. This was more than her husband could bear. He died soon after.

It was some years, indeed far too many, before a sentence was passed in the case. Pastor Nielsen was unfrocked. And not until 1649 were the charges against Kirstine withdrawn at the Herredags Court in Copenhagen. That same year the vengeful sexton had been reinstated in his old position. But two years later he threw himself from the very window in the belfry from which he had claimed to see the scandalous goings-on in the bishop's house. Rumour had it that he had committed suicide. It never became clear whether this was true; but at least people explained it as a just punishment for his false accusations that had caused the bishop's family so much misery.

Leyel must often have thought longingly of home. He cannot have imagined that he would have to remain so long in the East. But he had no ship fit for the long voyage home, nor could he leave the position entrusted to him. But there is little doubt that he would have been happy to leave if only it had been possible.

CHAPTER 12
REBELLION

Nevertheless, the opportunity to return home came before he expected it – and in quite a different way. In early 1648 there were signs of disagreement among the leading men at Dansborg. In February of that year Leyel asked Anders Nielsen to sail with the *St Peter and St Paul* to Macassar; but Nielsen refused and instead handed in a written request to be excused from this duty. The fact that Anders Nielsen writes to Leyel instead of discussing the matter with him seems to show that the good relations between the men had deteriorated. As the reason for his request he writes that he is afraid that the ship will have difficulties in reaching its destination as the monsoon is already almost over, i.e. the necessary west wind has died down. It is simply too late to make a voyage to the Islands. As an example of what this might mean he cites the voyage he made with Claus Rytter in *The Gilded Sun*. They set sail from India on February 23, 1642, but did not reach Bantam until June. Nielsen cannot think of that voyage without horror. Apparently they had suffered greatly, especially from the lack of water, and Anders Nielsen does not want to try that again. Perhaps he also feels old and tired, for he writes "I have now served out here in India for 12 years and have never requested to be spared from participating in any voyage or other journey".

It may be that the unrest was partly due to the new negotiations for peace with the Bengalis in the summer of 1647, which made Leyel stop the privateering voyages. This was hardly to the taste of most of the garrison as these were the sole opportunities for a little excitement and extra income.

The written sources do not show whether Leyel acceded to Nielsen's request. It is possible that he refused to give in. There was nobody else he could send. And now the privateering voyages had ceased he may have felt that the voyage to the Islands was the only way to make any profit. Nor was he apparently a man to sit passively at home. They had the ship and the goods and were familiar with the market – it was vital to keep going.

Apart from the privateering voyages that could offer some excitement, and, if they were lucky, a welcome addition to the monthly wages, the days were probably boringly monotonous, no matter whether one was at

Dansborg or at sea on the various routes they knew so well. There was no news from home, and one's comrades died one by one. A few of the men had married Portuguese or Indian women, had children and settled down. But others still longed for home.

It is dificult for us to understand what these men felt, completely cut off from their own country, hoping in vain year after year for a ship from home. The humid tropical heat, the diseases, the many deaths, the foreign peoples whose language and culture one hardly understood, the monotony, the oppressive loneliness. There was plenty to cause discontent.

As early as 1642 Claus Rytter had feared an armed rebellion among the men, though we do not know the details. But late in January of that year he wrote to Herman Clausen whom he trusted: "As to Mogens Pedersen and his followers. I hope they will yield before the game is up. As soon as Willem (not Willem Leyel) is on board again I will come ashore; I spoke to you of some of the locals if it became necessary to have them handy. Let Willem know that I will go ashore once he is on board. I will steal ashore without any shooting if you think it best. I know the man called Niels, but the other one I do not know for certain, for there are two or three." He also asks Clausen to send him a message telling him "how many people I need to take ashore with their arms, for I will not trust myself among them without my men." The exact circumstances behind this letter are not clear, but there seems to have been danger of an armed revolt led by some hotheads among the men.

Leyel, too, had some years before spoken of the unrest alwys lurking among the men and of his fear that it could lead to open mutiny. It is difficult to judge his ability as a leader of his men. He had restored order, repaired the crumbling fortress, and found means to reorganize the trade in spite of Pessart's huge debts, which he partly managed to settle. He established and maintained friendly relations with the nayak of Tanjore, the authorities in Ceylon, the Portuguese, and the English. Of all this there can be no doubt. He also had the vision to see new possibilities, suggesting to King Christian that he try to obtain permission to trade in the Philippines and to let other nations use Tranquebar as a base. He was apparently respected by the inhabitants of Tranquebar who came to his aid during his brief siege of Dansborg in 1644.

But how were his relations with the men under his command? Was he distant, strict, dictatorial? Eager to fill his own pockets without giving others a share of his good fortune? He seems not to have won the affection of his men. Had he become arbitrary and difficult to please? The entire garrison must have felt that Dansborg would soon pass into other hands. The Company would soon be history, and any hope of a pension or any kind of security in one's old age had drowned with the many ships and comrades lost at sea. And Leyel was not only worried about his own fate; he had a drunken wife and a small daughter at home, and a son, daughter-in-law and unknown grandchild in England who all looked to him for assistance.

The sources have no answers to all these questions.

It is possible that it was Leyel's attempt to insist on Anders Nielsen making the voyage to the Islands that finally sparked the revolt. But there is no doubt that it was Poul Hansen Korsør who was the ringleader; he maintained that Leyel had purloined money that rightfully belonged to the Company. One day when Leyel was not at home he seems to have seized the opportunity to look through his papers and found several he found interesting.

There was a small account book in which Poul Hansen thought he found proof that Leyel had appropriated money belonging to the Company. He consulted with Anders Nielsen and with Jørgen Hansen, who for so long had been captain of the *Christianshavn*. Perhaps they were all weary of Leyel's unfailing energy which continued to send them off on long voyages and reminded them that they should serve the Company loyally and well. But it seemed as though the Company was disintegrating, so why work oneself to death for something that no longer existed? And now Poul Hansen was telling them that while they were serving for such meagre wages Leyel was making his fortune by stealing some of the valuables from the prizes, money which rightfully belonged to the King.

At any rate, soon after Leyel returned from a voyage they arrested him in the name of the King and declared that he had been relieved of his command at Dansborg. It must have been distressing for Leyel to see that it was his most trusted men who had banded together to oppose him; besides Poul Hansen, it was all the men he had depended on: Jørgen Hansen Riber, Anders Nielsen, Nicolaj Samson, and Frantz Erkmand.

Leyel must have defended himself as well as he could and demanded to see the incriminating papers. He could explain everything. It may have been true that he had traded on his own account, but as things were, this could not be so grave a fault, and as they must all realize that the Company would hardly be able to pay them any kind of pension if they ever got home again, it was not unreasonable to think of the future.

None of the conspirators probably cared to hear his explanations.

The next few days they must have searched his rooms and his papers to find fresh material, enough to draft an indictment they could send home to the Company in Copenhagen. They packed all the incriminating evidence in a small chest and to prove that they were honest they made out a covering document: "The enclosed documents, papers, books, letters, and files are laid here just as they were found after the arrest of Señor Leyel, just as they are packed in this chest, small and big, bad and good, and nothing has been removed or added in any way that could serve to spare or blacken Señor Leyel. The only things removed from the said Señor Leyel's letters are the documents and letters necessary to demand the outstanding claims in various places, namely at Goa, Cochin, from Antony Carvalho, Joan del Meyda, and Roberto Wright.

"This paper signed and witnessed, actum the fortress of Danisborg, May 15 1648. Poul Hansen Korsør, Jørgen Hansen, Nicolaj Simonsen [Samson], Frandts Erkmand, Joannis Barnes."

On New Year's Eve the *Christianshavn* lay anchored off Bantam. Poul Hansen must have stayed at Dansborg to manage things there; but the other three conspirators – Johannes Barnes is not otherwise known – gathered to draft the indictment, where all the charges made against Leyel were set out in seven paragraphs. Unfortunately we no longer have the indictment. All we have are a few fragments:

"NOTA. Pro memoria. To wit these three bundles of Commander Willem Leyel's papers and documents:

A paper on which is written in Willem Leyel's own handwriting
61 17/32 ounces of gold……. Pardou 786
also 7 ounces 62 fano………..87 pardous 6 fano

Another half sheet of paper on which several expenses are noted, among these

that on March 10 was paid to Tiagepulle for the town's tribute 500 pardous and a note in the margin, His Majesty owes me these 500 pardous.

The said 61 17/32 ounces of gold are said to have been sold for 786 pardous, and this is the gold about which Willem Leyel's Canecapel (clerk) Teyapa has told us, as is written in our charges against and complaints of the said Willem Leyel under point 6.

The 7 ounces 62 fano gold will be found in the list, entered under the gold that was found in the possession of the said Willem Leyel.

3) Also another paper, Willem Leyel's invoice, lists what he has bought for himself in Bengal. Among other things it states that on January 4 1648, he has delivered to Mr Roberto Wright 11,530 pounds of Achin sulphur, and 400 tobacco pipes which the said Mr Roberto Wright was to sell for the said Willem Leyel. Furthermore, on 13 January it says that 2,880 pounds of Achin pepper have been delivered to Señor Antony Carvalho of Biblipatam which he was to sell for Willem Leyel's profit. The above sulphur, tobacco pipes, and pepper have been added together and the value put at 592½ pardous or real von achten.

"As Willem Leyel writes an invoice of 'the goods I have bought for myself in Bengal', then he must have bought these goods very cheaply or for false coins, for all these goods come from the two ships with the 23 elephants which we seized from the Moors in Bengal.

"When Willem Leyel is charged with purloining the above goods he should not be allowed to protest that he had taken them with the idea that it should belong to the King, his master, but, in truth, if he had continued in command these abovementioned goods and much else had found their way into Willem Leyel's own purse, and His Majesty seen none of it. Though Willem Leyel could on occasion lend His Majesty 200, and 3-, 4,- 500 pardou, which is likewise entered in Leyel's account books and his rough drafts, and then repay himself when it suited him. In this way Willem Leyel has obtained everything that is entered in his books and rough drafts, which from the abovementioned goods he had expected to get a profit with much more which we know and can be learnt from all his actions that in every way he has abused his duty and the oath he swore to His Majesty.

Actum the 'Christianshavn' off Bantam, December 31, 1648. Jørgen Hansen, Anders Nielsen, Nicolaj Samson."

This is all we know about the charges against Leyel. As so often history teases us with only half-told tales where we should like to know what really happened. Was Leyel really guilty of the charges? Or did his accusers merely want more freedom, perhaps to commit open piracy? On the other hand, it is true that the men behind the mutiny were no chance employees, but men who had been loyal supporters in all the Company's transactions in Leyel's time, men he had trusted and who had proved worthy of his trust.

It would seem that they sent the chest with Leyel's papers and the indictment home with a Dutch ship, and then afterwards set Leyel ashore at Bantam with enough money to carry him home.

The mutiny must have been a terrible blow. He had spent so many years of his life on this venture in the East, suffered so many hardships, illnesses, unbearable heat, and sleepless nights. He had dreamed of making Denmark a commercial power out here. But there had been so many difficulties to contend with. The endless delays on his voyage out; the governor of Tenerife who had done everything in his power to delay and ruin his voyage; the impossible Spanish bureaucracy at Madrid; his arrival at Tranquebar and the hopeless muddle Pessart had left behind him; the frustrating days when he lay with the *Christianshavn* off Tranquebar and could not gain admittance to the fortress the King had committed to his care; the drunken clergymen; his difficulties with the nayak; the wreck of *The Little Elephant*; the war with the Bengalis; the more and more exhausting attempts to manage without any assistance from home; the constant worries about the family at home and about his son in England who was asking for help – alas, what help could he, poverty-stricken as he was, now give any of them? He owned little more than the clothes he wore.

But in spite of all his difficulties there was now only one thing that mattered: to clear his name. In Copenhagen he was duly charged once he and the indictment had arrived. There are no records of the trial, but it looks as though the case was quickly abandoned for lack of evidence. It was only asssertions on both sides. Leyel had been highly esteemed by Christian IV, who was now dead, and those who knew him would have vouched for him, while nobody knew anything of his accusers. Leyel was of a well-known and respected family with many mayors to its credit, while all his accusers were ordinary men.

Presumably the new King Frederik III, or at any rate some of his men, listened to Leyel's account of conditions at Tranquebar and his hopes that the colony could manage until more ships could be sent out – if this would ever be possible. There were so many problems at home that Denmark had not the strength to think of anything so far away, and the Company had practically ceased to exist.

If Leyel could have seen into the future he would have been aghast to see that the first ship Denmark managed to send to Tranquebar did not leave until May 1669, twenty years after he had returned home. The miracle was that Dansborg was still in Danish hands. The mutineer Poul Hansen had proved equal to the task, though his methods were somewhat unorthodox, and his successor Eskild Andersen Kongsbakke continued the work. Roland Crappé and Leyel had marked out the trade routes, and by means of this trade along the coast and across the sea to the Islands, and as time went by, strongly augmented by privateering against Bengali vessels, or, indeed, pure piracy, they managed to earn enough to keep things going.

Old King Christian had had a hard time in his last years. So many of his plans had been wrecked, all his initiatives and the huge sums he had invested had led to nothing, nor had he been able to realize his dreams of making Denmark a great power. And in the summer of 1647 his heir, the appointed successor to the throne, had died. Indeed, of the eight sons he had had through the years, now only Anne Cathrine's youngest but one, Frederik, was left – all the others had died before Christian, and there had been plenty of quarrels, disappointments, even treachery among his daughters and their husbands.

But the tangible results of his reign stood there in Copenhagen, plain for all to see: the Round Tower, Rosenborg Castle, Holmen's big church, Nyboder, the King's new harbour with the arsenal and the victalling yard, Bremerholm with the great warships. And far away at Tranquebar stood Erik Grubbe's Dansborg, a lonely sentinel in distant lands.

Much had happened in Copenhagen while Leyel had been away. We can only guess that he found lodging either with his mother or sister Kirstine, who had now at last been cleared of the ugly accusations. His wife was probably past saving, if she was still alive, and he had no money for any of them. He applied to the King for enough to support his last years on account of his long service.

Frederik III took pity on him and in recognition of his long and faithful service he was granted such support:

"It is Our gracious will and pleasure that Our steward shall give Our well-beloved Willem Leyel in view of his humble petition from Our victualling store belonging to Our Castle in Copenhagen annually until We decide otherwise, to be reckoned from the last St Philip's and St James' Day the following victuals, that is rye 3 pounds, barley 4 pounds, butter 1 cask, beef two casks, pork 320 pounds, herrings 1 cask, cod 1 cask, oatmeal 1 cask, peas 1 cask, dried cod 1,320 pounds. From Our Castle in Copenhagen.

Haffniæ 22, Februari Anno 1654."

The fact that the King here uses the usual phrase "Our well-beloved Willem Leyel" must mean that Leyel had been cleared of any suspicion of fraud or swindle against the King or the Company. On the other hand, the reward for his years of labour must have been far from the great hopes with which he had left Denmark. He probably had had dreams of recognition and a coat of arms such as Roland Crappé had obtained for similar services. But here he stood and had to be grateful for the meagre bestowal of rations so that he could sustain his life.

A month later the dreaded bubonic plague came to Copenhagen from the Baltic ports in spite of prohibitions of any trade or commerce with them. People tried in vain to save themselves from the plague by fumigating their rooms with juniper, wormwood, or tar. But in July about 300 people were dying every week, and in August the number rose to 600. In all, about 8000 people died during the summer, and the church bells rang for funerals from dawn till dusk. The court fled from Copenhagen in April, and the University closed in May. Whether it was the plague that put an end to Willem Leyel's life we shall never know with any certainty; but it is likely that he was one of the many victims. At any rate he died in 1654.

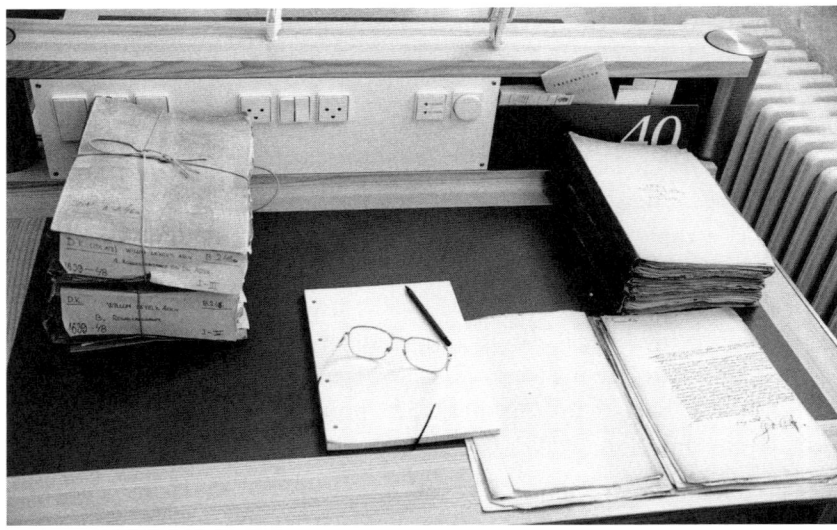

The Leyel documents in The Danish State Archives. There are three packages with Leyel's reports to the company in Copenhagen, letters in several languages, accounts from the ships and from Tranquebar, including customs receipts, and the record of the trials of the two clergymen, etc. (Photo: Kåre Lauring.)

When we look back at the accusations against Leyel today we must be thankful that the rebels sent him home with the indictment and a boxful of papers, for it must be precisely these papers, preserved in The National Archives, that give us the opportunity to gain some insight into Willem Leyel's life and the immense difficulties confronting the East India Company during these years.

These first thirty years, from 1618-48, laid a solid foundation for the East India Company's work in the East. In spite of all the difficulties the Company continued its work, though often at a reduced level. By means of a reorganization in 1670 the Company managed to keep going till 1729, and on the ruins of this old Company the so-called Asian Company was established, which existed until 1843. By a treaty dated February 22, 1845, Denmark ceded Tranquebar with the fortress Dansborg to the British East India Company.

Of the first leaders of the Company's trade in the East it was especially Roland Crappé and Willem Leyel, who managed to mark out the future pattern of trade and establish the necessary relations with the local princes and officials. Without their efforts the risky experiment could never have succeeded.

Ove Gjedde completed his mission and returned with a reasonable cargo, enough to make the shareholders feel it might be safe to continue. But it must be admitted that he would hardly have achieved such a good result without the vision and experience of Roland Crappé. The fortress of Dansborg became the tangible monument to this first expedition and still stands as a lonely sentinel by the Indian Ocean, though the waves are eating their way closer and closer to its walls.

The first three leaders of the Company in the East, Roland Crappé, Berent Pessart, and Willem Leyel had all first served with the Dutch East India Company, the VOC, where they had learned how best to establish a profitable trade here. Crappé and Pessart were both Dutch, whereas Willem Leyel was a Dane, born and raised in Elsinore. Without their knowledge of the trade routes, of the various currencies and units of weight and measure, and the local customs, languages, and culture, the Danes would not have had much success. It was also true that many of the mates, skippers, and merchants employed by the Danish Company were Dutch.

In spite of the assistance of these more or less experienced Dutch-men the Danish East India Company never lived up to the dreams that had launched this adventure. One cannot help asking whether the many shipwrecks that time and again helped to ruin the Company's finances were unavoidable, or merely a result of the fact that the Danes were ignorant of the storms, currents, and prevailing winds in the East.

But the reason why the expected profits never materialized was presumably that everything was done on too small a scale: too little capital with which to trade, too few ships, too few Danes at the important posts, too little discipline. The explanation of this is of couse that Christian IV's unfortunate wars wasted the country's resources to such an extent that he could not afford to invest enough capital in the Company. So that it gradually withered away so badly that it was a miracle that Dansborg was preserved in Danish hands for so long.

It is plain to see from the documents that daily life in the service of the Company was far from any romantic dream. The long voyages south around Africa and across the Indian Ocean cost many human lives, as did the heat, the many diseases, the isolation and homesickness at Tranquebar or the other trading stations. And many Danes were to find that life in these places disintegrated to end in drink and an unknown grave far away from home. The tale of the two drunken clergymen at Tranquebar in Leyel's time is merely one example of how bad things could get.

It is no surprise that the Danes out here were slave traders, nor was it only the Europeans who kept slaves; it was a custom of the times, and nobody seemed to find it wrong. Their piracy is more shocking – the seizing of Indian ships with their cargo was completely illegal and could presumably only partly be justified by the Indians' seizing goods from the Danish wrecks. At any rate, it developed into piracy pure and simple, gruesome as in the worst novels, when a Danish captain had the entire crew of a ship murdered after he had seized it in a privateering raid.

A somewhat mixed venture that started with magnificent visions of a Danish commercial enterprise. Huge sums of money disappeared almost without a trace in the Company's bottomless coffers; there were very few ships that returned home with the rich loads they had dreamed of; many shareholders must have lost their entire investment, and many men lost their lives and health in the Company's service.

But in spite of all these difficulties the Company undoubtedly had a not unimportant influence on people at home. Those who returned home like old Jon Olafsson gathered an astonished audience around them when they told of all their adventures in the East, so that many began to realize that there was a huge exotic world beyond the seas, a world it would be worth seeing at close quarters. There was an influx of hitherto unknown goods, spices, rice, Chinese porcelain, ivory, ebony, lacquerwork, cotton textiles, beautiful Persian carpets, and costly silks. Some men were seized with a longing for distant lands and the open spaces of the ocean and in the following years more and more ventured farther and farther abroad.

Men's horizons moved farther out as the world gradually seemed to grow larger.

BIBLIOGRAPHY

UNPUBLISHED SOURCES

The story of Willem Leyel is mainly based on materials deposited in The Danish State Archives (Rigsarkivet):

Willem Leyel's file (Danske Kancelli B 246, a, b, and c) consists of three packages of miscellaneous papers, a large part being accounts, such as expenses for the *Christianshavn*, for Leyel's stay at Tenerife and in Madrid, for tax revenues at Tranquebar, and a survey of the trade there. It also contains an account of the voyage to Plymouth, the ship's council's decision to seek a port of refuge in Santa Cruz, letters from the ship's officers to Leyel in Madrid, and his letters to the Company's men at Dansborg, to those on board the ships and to the galleys at Manila. There are a number of letters in the local languages, and in English, Dutch, Spanish and Portuguese; letters from Leyel's son Hans Leyel in England; the winding up of the estates of Herman Clausen and Christian Storm; and Records of the official examinations of the two clergymen. There also exist four long reports sent by Leyel to the board of directors in Copenhagen, dated April 16, 1644, November 22, 1644, December 12, 1645, and November 15, 1646.

Claus Rytter's voyage to India (Danske Kancelli B 245 a and b) consists of a number of miscellaneous papers, accounts, letters, reports of his trading ventures in India and of his voyage home with the impounding of his ship in England and his defense against the charge that he had been extravagant in spending money on gifts in the East.

The file of Asiatisk Kompagni, Tanjourske dokumenter 1620-78 (The Danish State Archives no. 2183a) has a few documents from the period.

Hannibal Sehested's letters and reports from Madrid (The Royal Library, Manuscript Department NKS 652, 2°) provides some information about Leyel's stay in that city.

Mourids Christensen's notes from Tranquebar date from a later period, but add some useful information (The Royal Library, Rostgaard 40.2).

Henning Engelhardt's "De ostindiske Etablissementers Historie" (Rigsarkivet, håndskriftsamlingen VII E 1 a) contains much information.

STUDIES AND REFERENCES

Bøggild-Andersen, C.O. *Hannibal Sehested. En dansk statsmand*, vol. 1. Aarhus 1970.

Cortemünde, J.P. *Dagbog fra en Ostindiefart 1672-75*. Henning Hennigsen (ed.). Elsinore 1953.

Feldbæk, Ole and Ole Justesen. *Kolonierne i Asien og Afrika*. Copenhagen 1980.

Holck, Harald. "Om Slægten Leyel", *Personalhistorisk Tidsskrift*, vol. 6, no. 13. 1958.

"Hr. Mads Rasmussens Reise til Ostindien 1623". *Danske Magazin*, vol. 4, 1745.

Kancelliets Brevbøger vedrørende Danmarks indre Forhold. Copenhagen 1919-1991.

Kong Christian den Fjerdes Dagbøger for Aarene 1618, 1619, 1620, 1625, 1635, udgivne, efter Originalerne, af R. Nyerup. Copenhagen 1825.

Kong Christian den Fjerdes egenhændige Breve. C.F. Bricka and J.A. Fredericia (eds). Copenhagen 1969-70.

Larsen, Kay. *Krøniker fra Trankebar*. Copenhagen 1918.

Larsen, Kay. *Dansk-Ostindiske Personalia og Data*. Copenhagen 1912.

Larsen, Kay. *De dansk-ostindiske Koloniers Historie I-II*. Copenhagen 1907-08.

Larsen, Kay. *Rebellerne i Trankebar*. Copenhagen 1907.

Larsen, Kay. *Danske Kapertogter i den Bengalske Havbugt*. Copenhagen 1906-7.

Niebuhr, B.G. "Nogle efterretninger om Wilhelm Leyel". Det *Skandinaviske Litteraturselskabs Skrifter*, vol. 1, 1805.

Ólafsson, Jon. *Islænderen Jon Olafssons Oplevelser som Ostindiefarer under Christian IV.* Memoirer og Breve, vol. 7. Copenhagen 1967 (1907).

Olsen, Gunnar. *Dansk Ostindien. Vore gamle tropekolonier*, vol. 5. Copenhagen 1967.

Schlegel, Johan Heinrich. *Sammlung zur Dänischen Geschichte*. Copenhagen 1772.

Slange, Niels. *Den stormægtigste Konges Christian den Fjerdes Historie*. Copenhagen 1749.

Sperling, Otto. *Notes du voyage en Espagne 1640-1641*. New York 1910.

Tønnesen, Allan. *Helsingørs udenlandske borgere og indbyggere ca. 1560-1600*. Ringe 1985.

Van der Chijs, J.A. et al. *Dagh-Register gehouden int Casteel Batavia vant passerende daer ter plaetse als over geheel Nederlandts-India*. Gravenhage 1887.

Willerslev, Richard. "Danmarks første aktieselskab", *Historisk Tidsskrift*, vol. 10, no. 6. 1944.

CHRONOLOGY OF EVENTS
IN LEYEL'S LIFE

(ca.) 1593	Willem Leyel is born in Elsinore.
1616	Establishment of the first Danish East India Company.
1618	March: Roland Crappé sails for Ceylon with the *Øresund*.
1618	November: Ove Gjedde's ekspedition leaves for Ceylon.
1620	Autumn: Ove Gjedde arrives at Tranquebar and begins to build Dansborg.
1620-37	Roland Crappé governor of Tranquebar.
1626	Willem Leyel and Claus Rytter at Pipeley.
1629	May 1: Willem Leyel appointed captain in the royal navy.
1635	November 19: The *Anna* and the *Jakob* leave with Crappé onboard the *Anna* and Leyel as chief merchant.
1637	January 16: The *Anna* leaves Tranquebar for Denmark with Crappé onboard.
1637	Crappé is knighted.
1637-44	Berent Pessart is governor of Tranquebar.
1639	November 8: The *Christianshavn* leaves Copenhagen with Leyel as commander together with *The Gilded Sun* with Claus Rytter as captain.
1640	March 3: The *Christianshavn* is detained at Santa Cruz.
1643	March 2: The *Christianshavn* is finally able to leave Santa Cruz.
1643	March 16: Claua Rytter leaves Tranquebar with *The Gilded Sun*.
1643	September 5: Leyel arrives at Tranquebar.
1644	June 11: Leyel anchors off Tranquebar and finds Dansborg closed to him.
1644-48	Willem Leyel governor of Tranquebar
1644	December: Dansborg attacked by General Tiagepule from Tanjore.
1645	January 30: Execution by drowning of Rev. Christian Storm.
1645	July: Berent Pessart is killed near Manila.
1645	October: Rev. Niels Andersen sentenced to death and exiled to Ceylon.
1648	Willem Leyel deposed by Poul Hansen Korsør and sent home.
1654	Spring: death of Willem Leyel in Copenhagen.